Kids on the Move Colorado

Every Parent's Guide to Traveling Around the State with Children

Fixed Pin Publishing

Laura Perdew

Errors may exist in this book as a result of the author and/or the people with whom they consulted. Because the information was gathered from a multitude of sources, they may not have been independently verified and therefore t**he publisher, or the authors, cannot guarantee the correctness of any of the information contained within this guidebook.**

THE AUTHOR AND PUBLISHER EXPRESSLY DISCLAIM ANY REPRESENTATIONS AND WARRANTIES REGARDING THIS GUIDE. THEY MAKE NO REPRESENTATIONS OR WARRANTIES, EXPRESSED OR IMPLIED, OF ANY KIND REGARDING THE ACCURACY OR RELIABILITY OF THE CONTENT OF THIS BOOK. THERE ARE NO WARRANTIES OF MERCHANTABILITY OR FITNESS FOR A PARTICULAR PUPROSE. THE USER ASSUMES ALL RISK ASSOCIATED WITH THE USE OF THIS BOOK AND ALL ACTIVITIES CONTAINED WITHIN IT.

Kids on the Move! Colorado by Laura Perdew

© 2012 Fixed Pin Publishing, LLC
All rights reserved. No part of this book may be used or reproduced in any manner without written permission from the publisher. Printed in China.
Front Cover: Enjoying a beautiful hiking trail outside the town of Aspen. photo by Laura Perdew

International Standard Book Number:
ISBN 978-0-9819016-6-4

Library of Congress Catalog in Publication Data:
Library of Congress Control Number: 2012939648

Fixed Pin Publishing is continually expanding its guidebooks and loves to hear from locals about their home areas. If you have an idea for a book, or would like to find out more about our company, contact:

Jason Haas
Fixed Pin Publishing
P.O. Box 3481
Boulder, CO 80307
jason@fixedpin.com

Ben Schneider
Fixed Pin Publishing
P.O. Box 3481
Boulder, CO 80307
ben@fixedpin.com

To my travel buddies: Cole, Jack and Pete

Also, a sincere thank you to Great Ourdoors Colorado, which "uses a portion of Lottery dollars to help preserve, protect, enhance and manage Colorado's wildlife, parks, river, trail and open space heritage." Their amazing work is in evidence across the state.

To learn more, please visit the author's website at www.lauraperdew.com

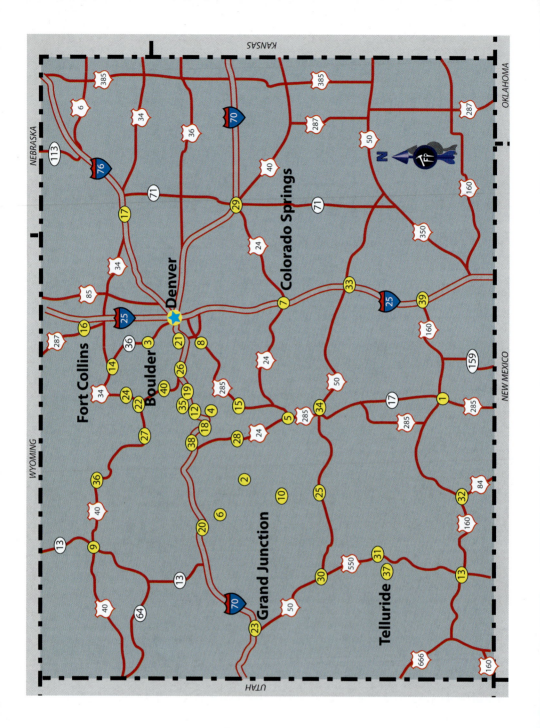

TABLE OF CONTENTS

INTRODUCTION 7

STOPOVERS

1. Alamosa 10
2. Aspen 12
3. Boulder 15
4. Breckenridge 19
5. Buena Vista 22
6. Carbondale 26
7. Colorado Springs 29
8. Conifer/Aspen Park . . 33
9. Craig 35
10. Crested Butte 38
11. Denver 42
12. Dillon 46
13. Durango 49
14. Estes Park 52
15. Fairplay 55
16. Fort Collins 57
17. Fort Morgan 61
18. Frisco 63
19. Georgetown 66
20. Glenwood Springs . . . 70
21. Golden 73
22. Granby 76
23. Grand Junction 79
24. Grand Lake 83
25. Gunnison 87
26. Idaho Springs 90
27. Kremmling 93
28. Leadville 96
29. Limon 99
30. Montrose 102
31. Ouray 105
32. Pagosa Springs 108
33. Pueblo 112
34. Salida 116
35. Silverthorne 119
36. Steamboat Springs . . . 122
37. Telluride 127
38. Vail 130
39. Walsenburg 134
40. Winter Park 136

APPENDICES

A. Top 10 Places to Stop and Play 139
B. What to Pack 140
C. Travel Tips 141
D. Games You Can Play . . 142

The beautiful backdrop to the incredibly fun Town Park, Crested Butte. photo: Nathan Pulley

INTRODUCTION

"Life is a journey, not a destination."
— *Ralph Waldo Emerson*

There is no doubt: having children changes your life. But it doesn't have to stop your life. Kids are portable. With the right planning and the right ideas, traveling with your kids can be a whole lot of fun.

This handy little guide is meant for parents traveling around Colorado by car. Each city or town listed is a good place to stop for a few minutes or a few days. The activities referenced here are meant to make the *journey* as exciting as the destination. A successful road trip is all about being willing to see new places and new things from the perspective of your child, and perhaps renewing your own sense of curiosity and wonder.

How to use this book (the 10 step guide):

1 - **Plan your trip**
2 - **Pack (see Appendix B)**
3 - **Drive**
4 - **Kids whine/cry/throw things/have to pee**
5 - **Try bribery, snacks, games (Appendix D), or singing**
6 - **Open book to the nearest town**
7 - **Find the best places to visit (and to go to the bathroom) in town**
8 - **Get out**
9 - **Breathe a sigh of relief**
10 - **Have fun!**

Each entry usually includes the following:

Blurb

Just a few facts to introduce you to the town you're in.

The Place to Go

Because, let's face it, sometimes you have to get out of the car FAST, and don't have time to wade through numerous choices. Each of these places is easily and quickly accessible from the main roads in town. They were also chosen because of what they had to offer, their uniqueness and/or their accessibility to other things (namely food and restrooms).

Parks

Many towns and cities had multiple parks to choose from. If you happen to have the luxury of reading this section, it will steer you to parks and playgrounds off the beaten path.

Splash Spot

A good kid-friendly spot by a creek or lake… no rapids, alligators, or steep drop-offs. This will keep kids entertained for as much time as you have to spare. Because, let's face it, kids love water.

Trails for Strollers & Little Folks

Need more than a run-around for the kids? These listings include possible places for a walk on paved or gravel paths with a stroller or small hiker. They were also chosen because they offer a lot to do…boulders to climb on, wildlife to see, a pond/creek to wade in or throw rock into, etc.

Kid-Friendly Eateries
(with something for adults too!)

Food, coffee, ice cream and even drinks… sustenance for weary travelers.

Things to do in Bad Weather

It's not always sunny, even in Colorado. But you still need to get out of the car. Many of the listings in these sections are recreation centers or museums that will get everyone out moving around.

Groceries/Supplies

Places in town to restock on anything you might need, from diapers to food.

More Info

For every town, this section includes the name and location of the local library; the nearest medical facilities; and the visitor center, because at some point you will find yourself in need of a book, a doctor, and more information than can be contained in these pages.

Other Fun Stuff

This part is for those that might want to stay longer in a particular town. It will include other places families might want to visit and other activities in town or nearby.

Directions

How to get there (which of course, you won't need if you're already there). Each town or city chapter also has an easy-to-reference map.

Parking

Oftentimes this isn't a problem, but in some cities, parking can be a real challenge. Check here for the most hassle-free options.

YE OLDE DISCLAIMER

Traveling with children in and of itself can be hazardous to your health. We take no responsibility for your sanity, but do hope that this book helps make your travels more fun.

On another note, as you visit towns and engage in various activities with your children, please be aware of the age and ability of your child. Some playgrounds are meant for older children. Some trails are multi-use, thus busy with bicyclists as well as pedestrians. Oftentimes water levels in creeks and streams are high, making them unsafe for wading. Rocks can be great for climbing, but not for everyone. Snacking in the car is a great idea, but be aware of choking hazards. You get the idea. Again, we take no responsibility, but do bid you happy trails, with a dash of caution.

Alamosa

"Adventure Starts Here"

Chances are if you're driving through Alamosa, you should stop, because there's a whole lot of "not much" in any direction for a long time. Think of it as a preemptive strike.

The Place to Go

Cole Park [A] - (At 3rd and Chamber Dr) What's not to love about a big open field, a shaded playground and an old train engine? Cole Park has it all, including public restrooms, a half-mile paved track that circles the park, and shaded picnic tables. Engine 169, which began working in the late 1800s on the Denver & Rio Grande Railroad, sits at the south end of the park. Thanks to the preservation efforts of the Friends of the 169, the engine is restored and on display for the public. Cole Park is also a short walk (a couple blocks) to the main drag.

Splash Spot

If you aren't experiencing a category 4 or 5 meltdown, and want a quiet spot, head north on State Avenue from Main Street. The mile drive will take you to a sheltered picnic table (with great views of the mountains) and an excellent place to splash in the water. [B]

Kid-Friendly Eateries
(with something for adults too!)

San Luis Valley Brewing Company [C] - 631 Main Street. (719) 587-BEER www.slvbrewco.com
Upscale pub-menu, and, of course, beer.

Milagros Coffee House [D] - 529 Main Street. (719) 589-9299 Good coffee, pastries, soups, salads, sandwiches.

Calvillo's Mexican Restaurant [E] - 400 Main Street. (719) 587-5500
Includes typical Mexican entrees, as well as a fresh buffet.

There are also many *fast-food* choices on the west of town on US-160/US-285.

Things to do in Bad Weather

The Inn of the Rio Grande Water Park [F] - 333 Santa Fe Ave. (Hwy-160) (719) 589-5833 or (800)669-1658 www.innoftherio.com/waterpark.html
Your kids will love you. The park has a 21-foot tall water slide, a kiddie frog slide for smaller swimmers, and three different pools to choose from (a splash pool, a recreation pool, and a kiddie pool). There are shower and changing facilities available, as well as a snack bar. $

San Luis Valley Museum [G] - 401 Hunt Ave. (719) 587-0667 www.museumtrail.org/SanLuisValleyHistoryMuseum.asp
The Museum has educational displays depicting early ranch and farm life, including a model post office, a typical country grade school classroom, and a mercantile. Visitors can also enjoy railroad memorabilia, artifacts of the culturally diverse settlers of the area, and a veterans' memorial wall honoring those who served in World War I and II. $

Groceries/Supplies

Safeway [H] - 1301 Main Street. (719) 587-3075

Alamosa

More Info

Library: Southern Peaks Public Library[I]
423 4th Street. (719) 589-6592
http://www.alamosalibrary.org/

Hospital/Emergency Care: San Luis Valley Regional Medical Center -
106 Blanca Avenue. (719) 589-2511
http://www.slvrmc.org/

Alamosa Convention & Visitors Bureau[J]
610 State Ave. (800) 258-7517 www.alamosa.org

Other Fun Stuff

Rio Grande Scenic Railroad[K] -
610 State Ave. (719) 587-0520 or (877) 726-7245
www.coloradotrain.com
If you have the time, take a ride on Colorado's historic rails across the valley and over scenic mountain passes, to old Western towns and vast wild places. $

Alamosa National Wildlife Refuge[L] -
9383 El Rancho Lane (719) 589-4021
www.fws.gov/alamosa/AlamosaNWR.html
This 11,169-acre refuge is a haven for migratory birds and other wildlife. Take a stroll along an interpretive trail, break out the binoculars to observe numerous kinds of birds, or spend time in the visitor's center. FREE

Great Sand Dunes National Park[M] -
Visitor Center: 11999 Hwy-150 Mosca, CO.
(719) 378-6399   http://www.nps.gov/grsa/
If you haven't been, you should go. For kids it's the largest sandbox they've ever seen. For adults, the dunes are a geologic marvel. And, if you're lucky, Medano Creek is flowing, providing endless hours of entertainment...for all of you. $

Directions

Alamosa sits more or less at the intersection of *US-160* and *US-285*, smack dab in the middle of the San Luis Valley (one of the largest high desert valleys in the world).

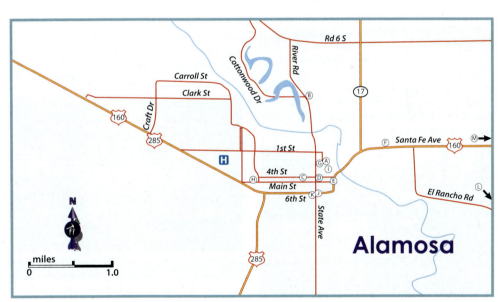

A. Cole Park – East end of town, 3rd and Chamber Dr
B. This shelter is one mile north of Main St, on State Ave, on the right, across from the golf course.
C. San Luis Valley Brewing Company – 631 Main St
D. Milagros Coffee House -529 Main St
E. Calvillo's Mexican Restaurant – 400 Main St
F. Inn of the Rio Grande Water Park – 333 Santa Fe
G. The San Luis Valley Museum – 401 Hunt Ave
H. Safeway – 1301 Main St
I. Southern Peaks Public Library: 423 4th St
J. Convention & Visitors Bureau – 610 State Ave
K. Rio Grande Scenic Railroad – 610 State Ave
L. Alamosa National Wildlife Refuge – El Rancho Lane (12 miles SE of Alamosa...from US-160 at mile marker 237, head south on El Rancho Rd)
M. Great Sand Dunes National Park – 11999 Hwy-150, Mosca, CO (follow US-160 east approximately 14 miles; head north on CO-150 all the way to the visitor center)

Aspen

Hard to believe now, but this small Victorian town began as a silver mining boom town in the late 1800s. Today the heart of Aspen is skiing, culture and outdoor recreation.

The Place to Go

John Denver Sanctuary & Rio Grande Park[A] - *(Mill Street and the Rio Grande Trail)* This is a great place to just stop. Park the car here, and it's an easy stroll to anywhere. The Aspen Chamber, the *Rio Grande Trail*[F] and more are nearby.

The sanctuary itself sits on the Roaring Fork River, paying tribute to the lyrics and life of John Denver. It's a peaceful place to relax, have a picnic, wade in the river, or start a walk.

Parking: There is a parking garage right next to the Aspen Chamber on Rio Grande Place. Other paid street parking is available.

Other Parks

Wagner Park[B] - (Mill Street and Durant Avenue) Right in downtown Aspen, Wagner Park is strategically located if you want to let the kiddos run around before or after some time downtown. There's a small playground, shade, picnic tables, and public restrooms.

Yellow Brick Park[C] - *(Bleeker & Garmisch, a block north of Main Street)* Another good stopping stop, a bit away from the downtown area. Yellow Brick Park has a playground, shade, picnic tables and public restrooms.

Herron Park[D] - *(Off US-82/Main Street at Neale Avenue, on the east end of town)* This park is on the Rio Grande Trail and the river. You'll find a shallow, sandy wading area that is popular with the local kids and dogs. If that's not enough entertainment, there is also a small wooden fort play structure, two swing sets and picnic benches. Public restrooms available.

Splash Spots

Try the *John Denver Sanctuary*[A] or *Herron Park*[D]. Also, along the *Rio Grande Trail*[F] there are dozens of great places to wade in the Roaring Fork River.

DeWolf / Fulton Fountain[E] (on the pedestrian mall) - Stop and dance with the water in this fountain on Hyman Avenue. Designed for kids of all ages, the water's pattern is set by a computer and software program designed by the late computer wizard Nick DeWolf.

both photos by Nathan Pulley

Trails for Strollers & Little Folks

Rio Grande Trail[F] - *(Head north on Mill St from Main St)* This trail is your best bet in town. It sits on the old Rio Grande Railroad bed, thus the name, and has a grade that never exceeds 3%. It is paved for the first 2 miles, then becomes a hard-packed surface. As you meander down the trail your kids will find dozens of places to wade in the river.

Aspen

North Star Nature Preserve [G] -
(1.5 miles east of Aspen) The 175-acre preserve is home to diverse wildlife, including several species of ground-nesting birds. There is an easy 3.2 mile loop through the preserve with great views of Independence Pass.

Grottos Trail [H] - *(9 miles E of Aspen on CO-82)*
If you're up for the drive, or heading in that direction anyway, this is a popular spot for exploring. The main trail crosses the bridge and heads left. Along the trail you'll find a waterfall, rock formations and an ice cave. Be sure to pack a picnic!

Kid-Friendly Eateries
(with something for adults too!)

Peach's Corner Café [I] - *121 S. Galena.*
(970) 544-9866 Stop in here for coffee, espresso, tea, smoothies or other breakfast and lunch items.

La Cantina [J] - *411 E. Main Street.*
(970) 925-3663 cantina-aspen.com
Delicious, unpretentious Mexican food at a good price.

The Big Wrap [K] - *520 E. Durant Avenue.*
(970) 544-1700 This is a locals' favorite, featuring gourmet wraps, tacos, salads and more.

Things to do in Bad Weather

Aspen Recreation Center (ARC) [L] -
0861 Maroon Creek Road. (970) 544-4100
www.aspenrecreation.com/aspen-recreation-centers/aspen-recreation-center/
The ARC has fun waiting for all of you. Of course the hit for the kids is the pool, where you'll find a lazy river and a two-story water slide. Outside, weather permitting, is access to trails. $

Aspen Center for Environmental Studies [M]
100 Puppy Smith Street. (970) 925-5756
http://www.aspennature.org/
This nature preserve and wildlife sanctuary sits on Hallam Lake and is a great place to learn about the wild side of Aspen. During the summer, programs include guided walks, children's programs, sunset beaver walks, and wild bird demonstrations. On your own you can explore the center inside, or follow the half-mile nature trail outside. FREE

Groceries/Supplies

City Market [N] - *711 E. Cooper Avenue.*
(970) 925-2590

Clark's Market [O] - *300 Puppy Smith Street.*
(970) 925-8046   www.clarksmarket.com

More Info

Library: Pitkin County Library [P] -
120 N. Mill Street. (970) 429-1900
http://www.pitcolib.org/page_1

Hospital/Emergency Care: *Aspen Valley Hospital* - *0401 Castle Creek Road.*
(970) 925-1120   avhaspen.org

Wheeler Opera House Visitors Center [Q] -
320 E. Hyman Avenue. (970) 920-7148

Other Fun Stuff

Silver Queen Gondola [R] - *(on Durant Avenue at Hunter)* (877) 282-7736   www.aspensnowmass.com/summer_rec/aspen.cfm
Unless someone's afraid of heights, the Silver Queen Gondola ride is a great family activity. It travels 2.5 miles to the 11,212-foot summit of Aspen Mountain. At the top, take in the scenery, go on a hike, or eat at the Sundeck. There are also guided nature tours, concerts, kids activities, disc golf and more. $

Aspen

Directions

The only major road through Aspen is US-82 from Carbondale or Independence Pass, so unless you're 4-wheelin', 82 will get you there.

left photo: Christopher Nowak, right: Nathan Pulley

A. John Denver Sanctuary – Follow Mill Street north from Main; on Mill and the Rio Grande Trail
B. Wagner Park – Mill St & Durant Ave
C. Yellow Brick Park – Bleeker & Garmisch
D. Herron Park – Main St (US-82) & Neale
E. DeWolf/Fulton Fountain – Hyman and S. Mill
F. Rio Grande Trail – Main St to N. Mill
G. North Star Nature Preserve – 1.5 miles east of Aspen on CO-82 and the Roaring Fork River
H. Grottos Trail – 9 miles east of Aspen on US-82, 1 mi past Weller Campground, trailhead on right.
I. Peach's Corner Café - 121 S. Galena
J. La Cantina - 411 E. Main St
K. Big Wrap - 520 E. Durant Ave
L. Aspen Rec Center – 0861 Maroon Creek Rd
M. Aspen Center for Environmental Studies – 100 Puppy Smith St
N. City Market – 711 E. Cooper Ave
O. Clark's Market – 300 Puppy Smith St
P. Pitkin County Library – 120 N. Mill St
Q. Opera House Visitor Center – 320 E. Hyman Ave
R. Silver Queen Gondola – Durant & Hunter

Boulder

Nestled at the base of the foothills, just below the Flatirons, Boulder is frequently referred to as "25 square miles surrounded by reality." Quirks aside, Boulder is an active, environmentally-friendly, artistic community.

The Place to Go

Pearl Streeet Mall[A] - Located between 11th and 15th Streets, the *Pearl Street Mall* is a perfect stopping spot for families with children; it has a little of everything and you only have to make one stop. For kids that need to move around, there are two play areas: rocks to climb on the 1200 block in front of Peppercorn, and animal sculptures to visit on the 1400 block near the Pedestrian Shops. In the summer, there is also a fountain running for kids to play in (on the 1300 block). Food choices span the spectrum (from a hot-dog cart to fine dining), including numerous places to eat outdoors and several coffee shops. Public restrooms are located at 13th and Pearl.

Parking: Paid parking is readily available along streets and in garages.

Park

Eben G. Fine Park[B] - *101 Arapahoe Avenue.* If you're not up for the bustle of downtown, try Eben G. Fine. Right along the banks of Boulder Creek, this playground has shade, picnic tables and public restrooms (open May-September). There are also numerous places to wade into the creek, as well as access to the *Boulder Creek Path*.

Splash Spot

Aside from *Eben G. Fine Park*[B], another great spot to wade in Boulder Creek is at the main branch of the *Boulder Public Library*[M].

16 Boulder

Trails for Strollers & Little Folks

Boulder Creek Path - This paved trail runs east-west for the length of the city along Boulder Creek. It is easily accessible from ***Eben G. Fine Park***[B] and the main branch of the ***Boulder Public Library***.[M]

Boulder Valley Ranch Open Space[C] - Just a mile outside of town, north on US-36 (turn right on Longhorn Road; trailhead is one mile down the gravel road, on the right), this open space has several gravel trails, many of which are stroller friendly. There's also an outhouse at the parking lot.

Chautauqua[D] - (900 Baseline Road) This park is just below the Flatirons and the views are spectacular no matter which way you look. There are dozens of trails to choose from, plus a playground just east of the dining hall. Picnic tables and public restrooms are also available.

Kid-Friendly Eateries
(with something for adults too!)

BJs Restaurant and Brewhouse[E] - 1125 Pearl Street. (303) 402-9294
www.bjsrestaurants.com
Pizza, pasta, sandwiches, a gluten-free menu and hand-crafted beer.

Salvaggio's Deli[F] - 1397 Pearl Street. (303) 545-6800   To-die for subs. Really.

Old Chicago[G] - 1102 Pearl Street. (303) 443-5071   www.oldchicago.com
Lotsa food choices, lotsa beer (as in, over 100 beers to pick from).

Southern Sun [H] - *627 South Broadway.*
(303) 543-0886   www.mountainsunpub.com
The place to go for the 30 to 40-something crowd with kids. Menu is mainly sandwiches and burgers. Beer is award winning.

Things to do in Bad Weather

North Boulder Recreation Center [I] -
3170 Broadway. (303) 413-7260
This rec center has a fantastic kid-pool, with a zero depth entry, slide for small kids, a tall, twisty water slide for bigger kids (and their adult!), and water works features. $

NCAR (National Center for Atmospheric Research) [J] - *1850 Table Mesa Drive.*
(303) 497-1000   www2.ucar.edu
The interactive displays at NCAR allow visitors to explore climate past and present, as well as consider future climate change. There are also hands-on exhibits in the Weather Gallery, science videos in the NCAR theatre, and the Walter Orr Roberts Weather Trail outside, just west of the building. FREE

Groceries/Supplies

South Boulder: King Soopers [K] -
3600 Table Mesa Drive. (303) 499-4004

North Boulder: Safeway [L] -
3325 28th Street/US-36. (303) 938-1271

More Info

Boulder Public Library – Main Branch [M] -
1001 Arapahoe Avenue. (303) 441-3100
www.boulderlibrary.org

Hospitals: *Boulder Community Hospital*
1100 Balsam. (303) 440-2273   www.bch.org

Boulder Community Foothills Hospital
4747 Arapahoe Avenue. (720) 854-7000   bch.org

Boulder Convention & Visitor's Bureau [N]
2440 Pearl Street. (Information is also available at kiosks on the 1300 block of Pearl Street)
(303) 442-2911 OR (800) 444-0447
www.bouldercoloradousa.com

Downtown Boulder, Inc. -
www.boulderdowntown.com

Other Fun Stuff

Walden Ponds Wildlife Habitat [O] -
East of town, near 75th and Valmont. www.bouldercounty.org/openspace/recreating/public_parks/walden.htm
Originally a gravel mine, Boulder County began a reclamation program at Walden in 1974 to create a wildlife habitat. Walden Ponds Wildlife Habitat was opened to the public in October 1975. Today there are 2.6 miles of trails, picnic tables and shelters, and public restrooms. This is a great place for a game of "I Spy" or a nature-oriented scavenger hunt (see Appendix D).

Chautauqua [D] - www.chautauqua.com
Not only is the park great for hiking, the Colorado Chautauqua is a national historic landmark, and a Boulder icon. Founded in 1898, this chautauqua is one of only three remaining in the United States. In continuous operation ever since, this gathering place brings people together for concerts, dance performances, lectures, art exhibits, and silent films. Guests can also dine at the Dining Hall, or choose to stay in one of the historic cottages or lodges.

Directions

From Denver head west on US-36. Exit at Baseline. Turn left at the end of the exit and drive west until you hit Broadway, then go right. This road will take you the length of town.

From Golden, take CO-93 north. This road becomes Broadway, leading you all the way to downtown.

From Longmont and Fort Collins, take CO-119 west. As you near the foothills, the road will hit Broadway. Go right to get to downtown.

Boulder

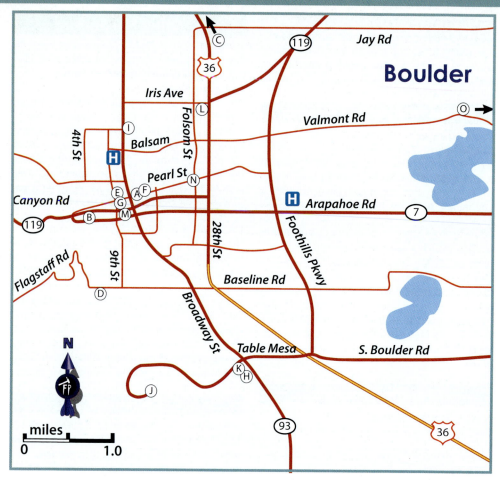

A. Pearl Street Mall – Pearl Street, between 11th and 15th Streets
B. Eben G. Fine Park – 101 Arapahoe Avenue
C. Boulder Valley Ranch Open Space - 1mi north of Boulder on Hwy-36, then 1mi east of Hwy-36 on Longhorn Rd (a dirt road). The turn-off from the highway onto Longhorn Rd is marked with a sign for Boulder Valley Ranch Open Space
D. Chautauqua – 900 Baseline Road
E. BJs Restaurant & Brewhouse – 1125 Pearl St.
F. Salvaggio's Deli – 1397 Pearl Street
G. Old Chicago – 1102 Pearl Street
H. Southern Sun – 627 S. Broadway
I. North Boulder Rec Center – 3170 Broadway
J. NCAR – 1850 Table Mesa Drive
K. King Soopers (S. Boulder) – 3600 Table Mesa Dr
L. Safeway (North Boulder) – 3325 28th Street
M. Boulder Public Library – 1001 Arapahoe Avenue
N. Boulder Convention and Visitors Bureau - 2440 Pearl Street
O. Walden Ponds Wildlife Habitat - East on Valmont, North on 75th

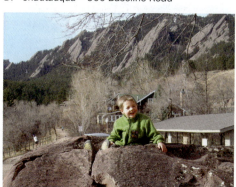

Breckenridge

Breckenridge sits at 9,600 feet, on the western slope of the Continental Divide. In this quaint Victorian town you'll find art, theatre, music, dance, shopping, recreational paths and more. And just at Breckenridge's back door are lush fields of wildflowers, raging rivers, endless trails and the soaring mountains of the Ten Mile Range.

The Place to Go

Blue River Plaza & Downtown[A] - (This is adjacent to the *Breckenridge Weclome Center* [M] at 203 S. Main.) Downtown Breckenridge is a happening place. It is a crossroads of culture, amenities and the great outdoors. The plaza has a small play area, public restrooms, and access to the river and the *River Walk*. From here you can also stroll through downtown.

Parking: Ample free parking street-side, and in marked public lots. Plus Free Ride buses operate continually within the town limits.

Splash Spot

Blue River Plaza[A] - While most of Breckenridge is along the Blue River, there's a great wading spot just west of the plaza. And chances are, you'll find others splashing around too.

Trails for Strollers & Little Folks

River Walk - The River Walk takes you the length of downtown (yes, along the river). It's a great place to go in Breckenridge, with the ski mountain to the west, shops to the east, the famed Riverwalk Center and even a small alpine garden along the way. Access at *Blue River Plaza.*[A]

Parks

Carter Park & Pavilion[B] - (South end of High St, by the elementary school.) This large town park takes you away from the downtown bustle. At the park are open spaces, a playground, picnic tables and public restrooms.

Kingdom Park[C] - (880 Airport Rd) This small park is tucked away in a quiet setting near the rec center. It offers a playground, picnic tables, public restrooms, shade and access to the *Blue River Bikeway*.

Breckenridge

Blue River Rec Path - This path is a small section of the world-class, 50+ mile paved Summit County Recreational Pathway system. The seven mile section in town is known as the Blue River Rec Path. It connects downtown with all of Summit County, and into Eagle County over Vail Pass.

Sapphire Point [D] - If you're up for a drive out of town (or if you're already heading in that direction) this is great trail for small children (those "hiking" on their own or those in carriers...strollers not recommended). The benefit for you is the remarkable view of Summit County. There is little to no elevation gain on this 1.6 mile hike.

Kid-Friendly Eateries
(with something for adults too!)

Breckenridge Brewery [E] - 600 S. Main Street. (970) 453-1550   www.breckbrew.com
If you like beer, this stop is a must. Oh yes, there is food for the kids, too.

Lucha Colorado Cantina [F] - 500 S. Main St. (970) 453-1342   www.luchacantina.com
Serving fresh tacos, burritos and more.

Rasta Pasta [G] - 411 South Main Street. (970) 453-7467
www.rastapasta.net/rasta-breckenridge.html
Pasta with a Caribbean flair for a great price.

Blue Moose [H] - 540 Main Street. (970) 453-4859
This breakfast place is a favorite among locals and returning visitors. The coffee's great, too.

Things to do in Bad Weather

Breckenridge Recreation Center [I] - 880 Airport Road. (970) 453-1734
www.townofbreckenridge.com
The center has two climbing walls, basketball, racquetball and tennis courts, swimming, and more. The leisure pool is a kid favorite with zero-depth entry, a large slide (big kids love this too!), a lazy river, basketball hoop and three play features. $

Mountaintop Children's Museum [J] - 605 S. Park Avenue. (970) 453-7878
http://www.mtntopmuseum.org/
They call this museum a "funtastic indoor place." There are several hands-on exhibits, including a Rocky Mountain Wildlife Exhibit, Creation Station, Kidstruction Zone, Wonder Lab, Mountain Top Medical Center and a Tot Spot (for the 2 and under crowd). $

Groceries/Supplies

City Market [K] - 400 N. Park Ave. (970) 453-0818

More Info

Summit County Library South [L] - 504 Airport Road. (970) 453-6098
www.co.summit.co.us/library

Hospital/Emergency Care: *High Country Health Care* - 400 N. Park, Suite 1A. (970) 547-9200   www.highcountryhealth.com

Summit Medical Center - 340 Peak One Drive, Frisco. (970) 668-3300
www.summitmedicalcenter.org

Breckenridge Welcome Center [M] - 203 S. Main Street. (877) 864-0868 or (970) 453-5579   www.gobreck.com

Other Fun Stuff

Peak 8 Fun Park [N] -
(970) 453-5000 or (800) 356-3972
www.breckenridge.com/peak-8-fun-park.aspx
Oh, darn, there's no parking at the base of Peak 8...you'll have to take the gondola. So jump on and ride to the top. The park has activities for all ages (summer only, of course): SuperSlides, putt-putt golf, a climbing wall, a human maze, a SuperBungee Trampoline and more. You can even take a guided hike. Gondola is FREE, activities are not.

Red, White and Blue Fire Museum [O] - 308 N. Main Street. (970)-453-9767
www.townofbreckenridge.com/index.aspx?page=423   The Red, White and Blue are actually three different fire companies that were organized in the late 1800s to protect the mining district in Breckenridge. The museum houses authentic fire-fighting equipment. What kid doesn't love fire trucks? FREE

Breckenridge

Directions

From the north, follow CO-9 south. From the south, do the opposite.

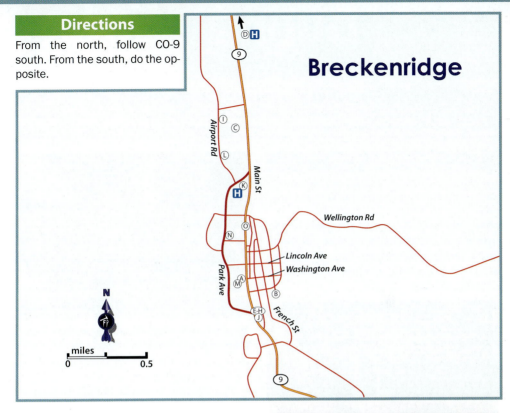

A. Blue River Plaza – On Main, next to the Welcome Center (203 S. Main)
B. Carter Park – four blocks east of Main Street, at the southern end of High Street (next to Breckenridge Elementary)
C. Kingdom Park – 880 Airport Rd., adjacent to the rec center (at the south end of the parking lot, near the ball fields)
D. Sapphire Point Trailhead - Drive 5 miles north on CO-9 to Swan Mountain Road. Turn right and drive 3mi to the top of the road; trailhead is on the left
E. Breckenridge Brewery – 600 S. Main Street
F. Lucha Colorado Cantina – 500 S. Main Street
G. Rasta Pasta – 411 S. Main Street
H. Blue Moose – 540 S. Main Street
I. Breckenridge Recreation Center – 880 Airport Rd
J. Mountaintop Children's Museum – 605 Park Ave
K. City Market – 400 N. Park Avenue
L. Library – 504 Airport Rd.
M. Breckenridge Welcome Center – 203 S. Main St
N. Peak 8 Fun Park - Parking is available in the Gondola South and Gondola North Parking Lots, along N. Park Ave near Watson Rd.
O. Red, White & Blue Fire Museum – 308 N. Main St

Buena Vista

"8,000 Feet above average"

If there's something you want to do outdoors in Colorado, you can do it from Buena Vista. Located in the heart of the Arkansas Valley, surrounded by the stunning Collegiate Peaks, this town offers everything from whitewater boating to hiking 14,000-foot peaks.

The Place to Go

Columbine Park [A] - (233 US-40) "Are we going to stop in Buena Vista?" my kids ask each time we're on a road trip 'cause they love this park. Columbine is a great stop, with shade, river access, picnic benches, public restrooms, and a fantastic playground. Plus, *K's Dairy Delite* [G] is next door, and frequently has outdoor BBQs as well.

Trails for Strollers & Little Folks

Barbara Whipple Trail [D] - Start at the *Buena Vista River Park* [B] and walk over a footbridge. The trail takes you through pinions on a gravel path to the old Midland train railroad bed. Great views of the Collegiate Peaks from just about any place on the trail. The kiosk near the bridge has trail info.

Arkansas River Trail - Also starting at the *Buena Vista River Park*, [B] this hard-packed trail runs north (where it intersects the Ripple Rock Trail) and south (to the new South Main development) along the west side of the river. The kiosk near the bridge has trail info.

Cottonwood Creek Trail - This trail, accessible from *McPhelemy Park*, [C] is an easy, hard-surface trail. It loops through town and near the Marquard Nature Area.

Splash Spots

Buena Vista River Park [B] - (eastern end of Main Street) This park, while designed for kayakers, is the perfect place for wading in the Arkansas. You can also watch the kayakers play, have a picnic, or take a hike.

McPhelemy Park [C] - (NW corner of US-24 and CR-306) This park has fishing at Town Lake (kids under 14 can fish for free!), restrooms, covered picnic tables, a small playground, the historic Railroad Depot (with a caboose visitors can tour), and access to trails.

Buena Vista   23

Kid-Friendly Eateries
(with something for adults too!)

Bongo Billy's Café E - 713 Highway-24 S. (719) 395-2634   www.bongobillyscafe.com
Coffee, pastries, soup, sandwiches and GREAT milkshakes.

Eddyline Restaurant & Brewery F - 926 S. Main Street. (719) 966-6000
www.eddylinepub.com   As they say, "The stoutest brew pub on the Arkansas River."

K's Dairy Delite G - 223 Highway-24 S. (719) 395-8695   What the heck, you're on vacation. Burgers and soft-serve ice cream for everyone!

Things to do in Bad Weather

Buena Vista Heritage Museum H - 506 E. Main Street. (719) 395-8458
www.buenavistaheritage.org
Housed in the old Chaffee County Courthouse, this museum includes a fashions room (for the style minded in your group), a commerce and industry room (for those with a business sense), and a schoolroom (for the kids!). There is also a display depicting the history of the railroad in the Arkansas Valley and a variety of art work. $

Jumpin' Good Goat Dairy I - 31700 Hwy-24 S. (719) 395-4646 OR (877) 994-2439   www.jumpingoodgoats.com
Well, now, this is different! Spend time touring the milking and cheese-making facility; visit with the goats; and taste lots of cheese. This dairy is committed to sustainable agriculture, and is one of the nation's fastest growing commercial cheese makers. Open April 1-October 1 for tours. $

Groceries/Supplies

City Market J - 438 Highway 24 South (719) 395-2431

More Info

Library: Buena Vista Public Library K - 131 Linderman Avenue. (719) 395-8700
www.buenavistalibrary.org

Hospital/Emergency Care: *Mountain Medical Clinic* - 36 Oak Street. (719) 395-8632 (Only open Monday through Friday)

Heart of the Rockies Regional Medical Center - 1000 Rush Drive, Salida (719) 530-2200
www.hrrmc.com

Buena Vista Area Chamber of Commerce L - 343 US-24. (719) 395-6612
www.buenavistacolorado.org

Other Fun Stuff

Mt. Princeton Hot Springs[M] - 15870 CR-162, Nathrop. (719) 395-2447 www.mtprinceton.com   Hang out in the river or in one of several pools of varying temperatures. The upper pool includes a lazy river and a very fast 300-foot water slide. A fun stop for the whole family! $

Mt. Princeton Hot Springs Stables[N] - 4582 CR-162, Nathrop. (719) 395-3630 www.coloradotrailrides.com   From short pony rides to long trail rides, you can find the perfect horse to suit each member of the family. $

Cottonwood Hot Springs Inn & Spa[O] - 18999 CR-306. (719) 395-6434 or (800) 241-4119 www.cottonwood-hot-springs.com   With many different soaking pools to choose from, the temperatures range from 94-100 degrees. This setting is quieter than Mt. Princeton Hot Springs, but the pools are strictly for soaking, not playing. $

Buena Vista

Directions

From the north, take US-24 south into town. From the south, do the opposite.

From the east, take US-285 west. When it intersects US-24, take a right and follow the road into town.

From the west, drop off Cottonwood Pass (on County Rd 306); this road becomes Main Street and intersects US-24.

A. Columbine Park – behind K's Dairy Delite, at 233 Highway-24 S
B. Buena Vista River Park – Take Main St. east until it reaches the dirt parking lot (veer to the left a bit) at the boat ramp.
C. McPhelemy Park – NW corner of US-24 and Chaffee County Road 306
D. Barbara Whipple Trail – See "B" above
E. Bongo Billy's – 713 Highway-24 S
F. Eddyline Pub – 926 Main Street
G. K's Dairy Delite – 223 Highway-24 S
H. Heritage Museum – 506 E. Main Street
I. Jumpin' Good Goat Dairy – 31700 Hwy- 24 N
J. City Market – 438 Highway-24 S
K. Public Library – 131 Linderman Ave
L. Chamber of Commerce – 343 Highway-24 S (in the white church with red trim)
M. Mount Princeton Hot Springs – 15870 CR 162, Natrhop, CO
N. Mt. Princeton Stables – 14582 CR 162, Nathrop, CO
O. Cottonwood Hot Springs – 18999 CR 306

Carbondale
"A Rocky Mountain Hideout"

Carbondale sits at the base of Mt. Sopris at the confluence of the Crystal and Roaring Fork Rivers. It's a little-known Colorado gem, and a quiet, beautiful place to stop.

The Place to Go

Downtown[A] - This is what's known as "one-stop stopping." From here you can access eateries, a playground, public restrooms, the rec center and trails.

Sopris Park[B] (7th and Main) The Park is right downtown, and the site of many town celebrations. It has large trees, a picnic shelter, a playground, and public restrooms. The *John M. Fleet Swimming Pool*[C] is also at this location.

Other Parks

Hendrick Park[D] - (CO-133 & Hendrick Road) There's space here for lots of running around, as well as a playground, public restrooms, and a trail that bisects the park.

Gianinetti-Sewell Park[E] - (Village Rd and Buggy Cricle) This is the closest park to CO-82 for those traveling that road and needing a quick stop. It is an all-organic park with shade trees, a playground, picnic tables, a nine-hole Frisbee golf course, and restrooms.

Splash Spot

John M. Fleet Swimming Pool[C] - 684 Main Street. (970) 704-4190
The pool is open during the summer months only, but after a hot day in the car, a splash in the pool sounds great! $

Trails for Strollers & Little Folks

Rio Grande Trail[F] - The trail parallels downtown, and if you are so inclined will take you all the way to Glenwood Springs to the northwest, or Aspen to the southeast. It is part of the Rails-to-Trails effort, turning old tracks into pedestrian and bike paths through the Roaring Fork Valley. www.rfta.com/trailmap.pdf

photos by Nathan Pulley

Carbondale

Kid-Friendly Eateries
(with something for adults too!)

Mi Casita [G] - *580 Main Street.*
(970) 963-5866   www.mi-casita.net
You guessed it...Mexican food (and home to the valley's famous "turborita"!)

Peppino's Pizza [H] - *524 Main Street. (970) 963-2993   www.peppinospizzacarbondale.com*
This no frills, walk-up order pizza place is a locals' favorite.

The Lift Coffee Shop [I] - *433 Main Street (970) 963-0573*
Paninis, smoothies, and sweet treats.

Fatbelly Burgers [J] - *220 Main Street (970) 963-1569   www.fatbellyburgers.com*
Grab and go burgers, dogs, and a little something for veg heads.

Things to do in Bad Weather

Carbondale Recreation & Community Center [K] - *567 Colorado Avenue. (970) 704-4190*
Burn off some energy in the gymnasium! They throw out balls and scooters and such for kids to play with. "Play Care" is also available in the mornings for children 1-8 years old while their adults use the facility. Outside you'll also find a lovely botanical garden and gravel path. $

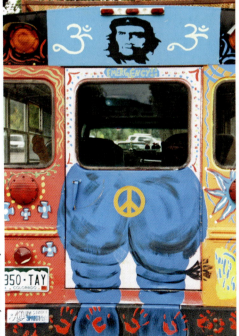
photo by Nathan Pulley

Mt. Sopris Historical Society [L] -
Museum: Weant & CO-133. (970) 963-7041
www.mtsoprishistoricalsociety.org
Visit an authentic homesteader's cabin, built in the 1880s. On display are tools, photos and household items. This is also a good place to start the walking tour of historic downtown Carbondale. FREE

Groceries/Supplies

City Market - Food and Pharmacy [M] -
1051 Highway-133. (970) 963-3255

More Info

Library: Gordon Cooper Library [N] -
76 S. 4th Street. (970) 963-2889
www.garfieldlibraries.org

Hospital/Emergency Care: *Aspen Valley Hospital* - *0401 Castle Creek Rd., Aspen (970) 925-1120   www.avhaspen.org*

Chamber of Commerce -
981 Cowen Drive, Suite C. (970) 963-1890
www.carbondale.com

Other Fun Stuff

Penny Hot Springs [O] - *(Look for a turnout on the east side of CO-133 a few hundred feet north of mile marker 55, about 15 miles south of town)*
This hot spring is a fun surprise for the whole family. The kids get to play in the Crystal River, and the adults get to relax. Water temperatures are scalding at times, but you can add or remove rocks to regulate the "pools" created by previous bathers. There is no caretaker, nor are there restrooms or a bathhouse, but this is part of what makes it unique. The unwritten ethic is to leave the area cleaner than you found it. FREE

Directions

From the south, take CO-133. This road will intersect Main Street.

Traveling from Glenwood Springs or Aspen on CO-82, take CO-133 south to get to downtown.

Carbondale

photo by Nathan Pulley

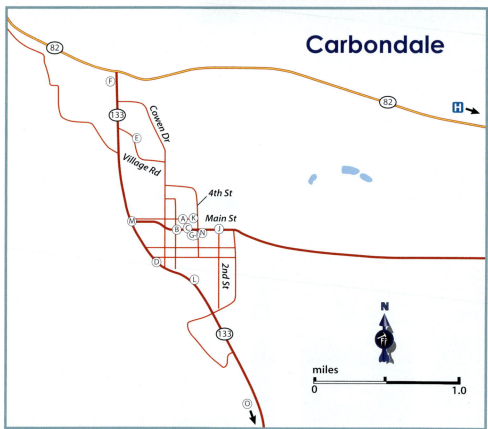

A. Downtown – from CO-133 turn east onto Main St
B. Sopris Park – 7th and Main
C. John M. Fleet Swimming Pool – 684 Main Street
D. Hendrick Park – CO-133 & Hendrick Road
E. Gianinetti-Sewell Park – Village Rd & Buggy Circle
F. Rio Grande Trail – Park either at the Carbondale Park & Ride (on CO-133 just south of CO-82), or at the rec center
G. Mi Casita – 580 Main Street
H. Peppino's Pizza – 524 Main Street
I. The Lift – 433 Main Street
J. Fatbelly Burgers – 220 Main Street
K. Carbondale Rec Center – 567 Colorado Ave
L. Mt. Sopris Historical Society – intersection of Weant Blvd and CO-133
M. City Market – 1051 Highway 133
N. Gordon Cooper Library – 76 S. 4th Street
O. Penny Hot Springs – just north of mile marker 55 on CO-133, 15 miles south of town

Colorado Springs

"The Springs" is very much a big city. However, a closer look reveals an extensive park and trail system, outdoor recreation opportunities and diverse cultural opportunities. Really, stopping here is a nice surprise.

The Place to Go

Memorial Park[A] - *(best access is off S. Union Boulevard, or Pikes Peak Avenue)*
Memorial Park is an oasis with something to offer just about everyone: three playgrounds, sandy areas for wading in Prospect Lake, the Prospect Lake fitness trail and other jogging trails, fishing areas, sports fields, picnic tables and shelters, public restrooms, and more.

photo by Nathan Pulley

Other Parks

Monument Valley Park[B] - *(access to the north end off Monroe St and Wood Ave; south end access from W. Bijou St and Sierra Madre St)*
At both ends of this long, skinny park are playgrounds and picnic shelters. You'll also find walking and biking paths, a fitness trail, access to the *Pikes Peak Greenway Trail* (more info below), wading spots in Monument Creek, two fishing ponds, shade, open spaces and public restrooms. In addition, the Horticultural Art Society Demonstration Gardens and City Greenhouse are in the park.

America the Beautiful Park (formerly Confluence Park)[C] - *(best access from Colorado Avenue, just west of S. Sierra Madre Street)*
A quick jaunt off I-25 lands travelers in this beautiful park. Not only is there shade, grassy areas, picnic tables, a playground, trails, restrooms, access to the *Pikes Peak Greenway*, but also the Julie Penrose Fountain. The O-shaped fountain, which represents the life-giving movement of water, operates in the summer from 10:00am to 5:00pm.

Splash Spots

Uncle Wilbur's Fountain - Acacia Park[D]
(Tejon & Bijou Streets) This was the first park in the Springs, donated by General William Jackson Palmer. Uncle Wilbur's Fountain is a favorite with the kids (and their adults!) on hot days. The park also has a small playground, picnic tables, public restrooms, and shuffleboard.

Prospect Lake in *Memorial Park*[A].

Monument Creek in *Monument Valley Park*[B].

Trails for Strollers & Little Folks

Memorial Park[A] - This enormous city park has numerous paths, including one around Prospect Lake.

Pikes Peak Greenway - This path is the primary north-south trail through the Springs, totaling 16 miles. It takes you not only across the city on concrete, asphalt and gravel surfaces, but also through many parks. Easy access and parking at both *Monument Valley Park*[B] and *America the Beautiful Park*[C].

Colorado Springs

photo by Nathan Pulley

Kid-Friendly Eateries
(with something for adults too!)

Phantom Canyon Brewery [E] -
2 E. Pikes Peak Avenue. (719) 635-2800
www.phantomcanyon.com
Oh, so much beer to choose from, so little time.

OPB&J Restaurant [F] - 3 E. Bijou Street.
(719) 571-9443   A gourmet PB&J sandwich? See for yourself.

Wooglin's Deli & Café [G] - 823 N. Tejon Street.
(719) 578-9443   www.wooglinsdeli.com
Serves breakfast, lunch and dinner, including locally roasted coffee and home-baked desserts. This deli won "Best of Colorado Springs" four consecutive years!

Things to do in Bad Weather

Firefighter Musuem [H] - 375 Printers Parkway.
(719) 385-5950   www.fire-museum.com
Oh, fire trucks! The Hook and Ladder Company No. 1 began protecting Colorado Springs in 1872. The rest is history, chronicled in the museum. FREE

Colorado Springs Pioneer Museum [I] -
215 S. Tejon Street. (719) 385-5990
www.cspm.org
Located in the renovated El Paso County Court House, the museum preserves the history and culture of the Pikes Peak region. FREE

Colorado Springs Recreation Center [J] -
280 S. Union Boulevard. (719) 385-5984
www.csreccenter.com
The center features an indoor pool and a 10,000 square foot fitness area open daily. The pool includes a zero-entry, current river, bubble couch, play area, and water slide. Best of all, the temperature is kept at 87°. $

Manitou Swimming Pool & Fitness Center [K] - 202 Manitou Avenue, Manitou Springs.
(719) 685-9735   www.manitoupool.com
Recently renovated and updated, the 83-degree pool will make everyone happy (and burn some energy!). $

Colorado Springs 31

photos by Nathan Pulley

Groceries/Supplies

King Soopers^L - 1750 W Uintah Street. (719) 636-5043

Safeway^M - 1920 S. Nevada Ave. (719) 636-5255

More Info

Library: Penrose Public Library^N - 20 N. Cascade Avenue. (719) 531-6333
http://www.ppld.org/

Hospitals: *Memorial Hospital* - 1400 E Boulder Street.
(719) 365-5000   www.memorialhealthsystem.com

Penrose St. Francis Hospital - 2222 N. Nevada Avenue. (719) 776-5000
www.penrosestfrancis.org

Colorado Springs Convention and Visitors Bureau^O - 515 S. Cascade Avenue.
(719) 635-7506 OR (800) 368-4748
www.visitcos.com

Other Fun Stuff

Garden of the Gods^P - 1805 North 30th Street.
(719) 634-6666   www.gardenofgods.com
If you haven't been, it might be worth the stop. Garden of the Gods is a registered National Natural Landmark, and a geological marvel of 300-foot sandstone rock formations sitting against the backdrop of Pikes Peak. Drop by the Visitor & Nature Center to find out more about the formation of the red rocks, and trails through the area. FREE

US Olympic Training Center^Q -
1 Olympic Plaza. (888) 659-8687
www.teamusa.org/about-usoc/u-s-olympic-training-center-colorado-springs/tours
For Olympics fans and sports enthusiasts, the Olympic Visitor Center includes the U.S. Olympic Hall of Fame Rotunda, a collection of memorabilia, interactive kiosks, tours, a store and more. FREE

Pikes Peak Cog Railway R-

515 Ruxton Avenue, Manitou Springs.
(719) 685-5401   www.cograilway.com

Ride to the top of Pikes Peak by train! The railway is fun for kids, and the ride is relaxing for adults. The train takes passengers through four life zones and abundant wildlife to the peak that inspired the song, "America the Beautiful." Open year round. $

Directions

Interstate 25 is the main artery north-south.

From the west, US-24 will bring you right into the heart of the city.

A. Memorial Park – 1605 E. Pikes Peak Avenue
B. Monument Valley Park - 170 W. Cache La Poudre St
C. America the Beautiful Park – 126 Cimino Dr.
D. Acacia Park – 115 E. Platte Avenue
E. Phantom Canyon Brewery – 2 E. Pikes Peak Avenue
F. OPB&J Restaurant - 3 E Bijou Street
G. Wooglin's Deli & Café – 823 N. Tejon Street
H. Firefighter Museum – 375 Printers Parkway
I. CO Springs Pioneer Museum – 215 S. Tejon St
J. CO Springs Rec Center - 280 S. Union Blvd.
K. Manitou Swimming Pool and Fitness Center – 202 Manitou Avenue, Manitou Springs
L. King Soopers – 1750 W. Uinta Street
M. Safeway – 1920 S. Nevada Avenue
N. Penrose Public Library – 20 N. Cascade Ave
O. CO Springs Convention & Visitors Bureau - 515 South Cascade Avenue
P. Garden of the Gods – 1805 North 30th Street. From I-25, take exit 146 (Garden of the Gods Rd) and head west for 2.5 m; turn left onto 30th Street. Visitor center is about 1 mile down on the left.
Q. US Olympic Training Center – 1 Olympic Plaza
R. Pikes Peak Cog Railway – 515 Ruxton Avenue, Manitou Springs

Conifer/Aspen Park

"An Ideal Place to Live"

Located just 15 miles southwest of Denver in the foothills, Conifer is a town proud of its diversity, and it is surrounded by aspen trees (ironic, isn't it?), Jefferson County Open Space Parks and the Colorado Rockies.

The Place to Go

Conifer Community Park [A] -
11369 Foxton Road. (303) 838-3705
www.conifercommunitypark.org
Located just a half-mile from US-285, this park is a great find. The 450-acre open-space park sits amid meadows, rolling hills, forests and creeks. You'll find five miles of trails, a disc-golf course, a picnic area, a small playground, and an outhouse.

Another Park

West Jefferson Elementary (Aspen Park) [B]
26501 Barkley Road. If someone really needs to get out of the car, this is a good bet because it's right off the road. Open to the public during non-school hours, it doesn't have much in the way of amenities, but the kids will have fun on the playground (and that is what's important!).

Splash Spot

Reynolds Park Open Space [C] - If you want water and quiet, the five-mile drive down Foxton Road is worth it. There are numerous places right near the parking lot to dip a toe or two, as well as several nicely shaded, secluded picnic tables. Public restrooms available.

Trails for Strollers & Little Folks

Valley Trail [D] - This hard-packed surface literally runs through the valley at the ***Conifer Community Park***.[A] Total length 1.5 miles.

Songbird Trail [E] - Try this short, level trail in ***Reynolds Park***.[C] It follows the stream bed and is ideal for little legs. Many other trail choices can lengthen the hike.

Kid-Friendly Eateries
(with something for adults too!)

Aspen Perk Coffee House [F] - *25797 Conifer Rd, Suite B102. (303) 816-4339*
A comfy, local coffee house with good coffee, pastries and breakfast.

Sonic Drive-In [G] - *Conifer Town Center 27171 Main Street. (303) 816-0056.* Burgers.

Starbucks Drive-Thru [H] - *26724 Conifer Town Center Drive. (303) 838-4924*

Conifer/Aspen Park

Things to do in Bad Weather

Choices are limited. You could, **A)** keep driving; **B)** stop at a restaurant; **C)** break out the raincoats and go for a rain hike; or **D)** try a scavenger hunt in the grocery store (see Appendix D).

Groceries/Supplies

King Soopers: Aspen Park[I] - 25637 Conifer Road. (303) 816-4960

Safeway: Conifer Town Center[J] - 27152 Main Street. (303) 838-4375

More Info

Library: Conifer Library[K] - 10441 Hwy-73. (303)235-5275 jefferson.lib.co.us/locations/cf.html

Hospital/Emergency Care: *Conifer Medical Center* - 26659 Pleasant Park Road. (303) 647-5300 www.conifermed.com

Visitor's Center: Conifer Area Chamber of Commerce[L] - (303) 838-5711
www.goconifer.com

Conifer Community Park Office[A] - 11369 Foxton Road. (303) 838-3705
www.conifercommunitypark.org
While this office is technically there for the community park, it's stocked with local brochures, maps and other info.

Directions

If you're passing through Conifer and Aspen Park, you're most likely on US-285. It's the main road north-south.

From Evergreen, take CO-73 south.

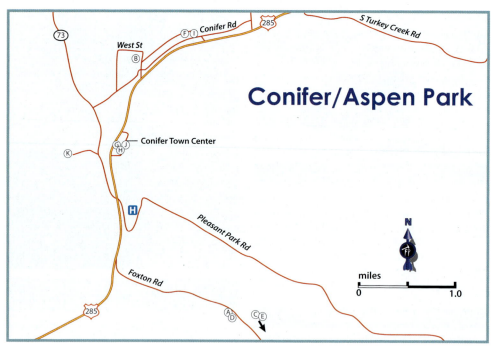

A. Conifer Community Park – 11369 Foxton Rd
B. West Jefferson Elementary – 26501 Barkley
C. Reynolds Park Open Space – 5.5 miles south on Foxton Rd.; park on the right
D. Valley Trail – TH at Conifer Community Park
E. Songbird Trail – Trailhead in Reynolds Park
F. Aspen Perk Coffee House – 25797 Conifer Rd., Suite B102 (Aspen Park)
G. Sonic – 27171 Main St (Conifer Town Center)
H. Starbucks - 26724 Conifer Town Centre Dr
I. King Soopers – 25637 Conifer Rd (Aspen Park)
J. Safeway – 27152 Main St (Conifer Town Center)
K. Conifer Library – 10441 Highway 73

Craig

"The land of rugged adventure and rugged landscapes"

This little town is an oasis in the middle of a lot of open space and really big sky. If you're heading west, it's also the last stop for a long, long time.

The Place to Go

City Park [A] - (Victory Way and Washington St)
City Park is the perfect stop for a quick break. There's plenty of shade, picnic tables, a public restroom and two playgrounds to choose from. For smaller kids, stop at the south end, amongst the numerous chainsaw-carved wooden sculptures. The bigger playground is past the swimming complex on the north end of the park.

Splash Spots

Loudy Simpson Park [B] - *500 S. Ranney Street. www.craig-chamber.com/community-facilities.html*
On the Yampa River, Loudy Simpson Park includes a two-mile trail that loops around the park, a nature trail, a disc golf course, two playgrounds, picnic tables and public restrooms. There is also river access here.

Craig Swimming Complex [C] -
605 Washington Street. (970) 824-3015
Surfing in Colorado? Yes, in Craig! This pool is one of only two wave pools on the Western Slope. Kids of all ages can enjoy the waves, as entry begins at zero-depth. There is also a six-lane L-shaped pool with diving boards.

Trails for Strollers & Little Folks

Loudy Simpson Park [B]

Kid-Friendly Eateries
(with something for adults too!)

Carelli's Inc [D] - 465 Yampa Avenue. (970) 824-6868   Serving pasta, pizza, Italian subs, calzones and more.

Vallarta's [E] - 1111 W. Victory Way. (970) 824-9812   Authentic Mexican food.

Serendipity Coffee Shop [F] - 576 Yampa Avenue. (970) 824-5846   Coffee, etc.

There are also numerous *fast-food* choices on the west end of town.

Things to do in Bad Weather

Museum of Northwest Colorado [G] - 590 Yampa Avenue. (970) 824-6360 www.museumnwco.org   The old west lives on in the museum's world-class collection of cowboy and gunfighter artifacts. Other exhibits include an old schoolroom, a hardware store, Native American artifacts, and miner and farm displays. FREE

Wyman Living History Museum [H] - 94350 US-40 (4 miles east of Craig). (970) 824-6346   www.wymanmuseum.com They guarantee you'll see something you've never seen before in the eclectic displays spanning over 100 years of American life. Start at the Colorado license plate collection and end at the premiere chain-saw exhibit. Along the way you can visit the bank, the store and your grandmother's kitchen! FREE

Groceries/Supplies

Safeway [I] - 1296 W. Victory Way. (970) 824-9496

City Market [J] - 505 W. Victory Way. (970) 824-6515

More Info

Moffat County Library [K] - 570 Green Street. (970) 824-5116   www.moffat.lib.co.us

Hospital/Emergency Care: *The Memorial Hospital* - 750 Hospital Loop Road. (970) 824-9411   www.thememorialhospital.com

Craig Chamber of Commerce & Moffat County Visitor Center [L] - 360 E. Victory Way. (970) 824-5689 OR (800) 864-4405 www.craig-chamber.com

Moffat County Tourism www.moffatcountytourism.com

Other Fun Stuff

Elkhead Reservoir [M] - 10 miles northeast of Craig on CR-29 www.craig-chamber.com/Elkhead-Reservoir.html Located 10 miles northeast of Craig, this reservoir offers a beach, swimming and 11 miles of trails (accessed at the Elkhead parking area, Greenwood's Cover, Cedar Bend or East Beach).

Directions

US-40 runs east-west right through town.

CO-13 will bring you into town from the north or south.

Craig

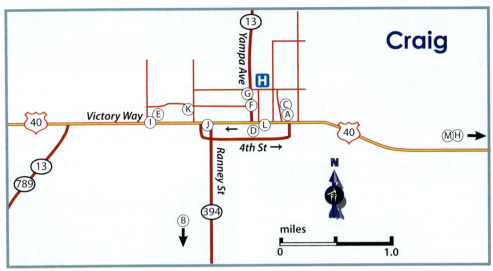

A. City Park – US-40/E. Victory Way & Washington St
B. Loudy Simpson Park – 500 S. Ranney Street
C. Swimming Complex – 605 Washington St
D. Carelli's – 465 Yampa Ave
E. Vallarta's – 1111 W. Victory Way, #114
F. Serendipity Coffee Shop – 576 Yampa Ave
G. Museum of NW Colorado – 590 Yampa Ave
H. Wyman Living History Museum – 94350 US-40
I. Safeway – 1296 W. Victory Way
J. City Market – 505 W. Victory Way
K. Moffat County Library – 570 Green Street
L. Chamber of Commerce & Moffat County Visitor Center – 360 E. Victory Way
M. Elhead Reservoir - 10 miles northeast of Craig on CR-29

Crested Butte

Okay, so most folks don't just "pass through" Crested Butte. But it sure is a great place to stop. Nestled in the heart of the West Elk Range, Crested Butte is surrounded by stunning peaks and brilliant wildflowers. The town is one of the few remaining true Colorado ski towns, and prides itself on its small town charm and adventurous spirit.

The Place to Go

Town Park[A] - *(Just north of the Center for the Arts, on 6th/CO-135 at Whiterock Ave)* This is a great place to stop because it is also close to downtown. In the park there is a picnic pavilion, two large playgrounds, shade, open fields and public restrooms. Run the kids around for a while, then stroll down Elk Avenue, which is the main artery for downtown Crested Butte.

Another Park

Rainbow Park[B] - *(Maroon & 8th)* This large, brand new park sits just below the towering Mt. Crested Butte. It's off the main drag, but still only a few blocks from downtown. There's a huge playground and picnic pavilion, as well as ball fields and public restrooms.

Splash Spot

Slate River Road: Oh-Be-Joyful Picnic/ Camping Area[C] - *(3.4mi west on Slate River Rd)* The short drive out of town is worth it. Not only is it beautiful, but it's a fun spot for chucking rocks into the water or wading if it's not too cold. Also a good place for a picnic or hike.

Trails for Strollers & Little Folks

The Rec Path (connecting CB with Mt CB)[D] In Crested Butte, access this trail from the east end of Teocali Avenue, just over the footbridge crossing the Slate River. The paved path connects Crested Butte with Mount Crested Butte, and winds through meadows, wetlands and spectacular scenery.

Peanut Lake/Lower Loop[E] - *(At edge of town take Butte Ave/Peanut Lake Rd west for 1.1 mi to a small parking lot on the left)* Start your hike by tiptoeing over the cattle guard, then follow the road to the right. This is a great beginner trail, and if you walk far enough you'll find places to throw rocks into the river, or to get in.

Crested Butte 39

Kid-Friendly Eateries
(with something for adults too!)

The Brick Oven Pizzeria & Pub[F] - 223 Elk Avenue. (970) 349-5044
www.brickovencb.com   Enjoy pizza, subs, pasta and drinks. Gluten-free items available.

Camp 4 Coffee[G] - 402 ½ Elk Avenue.
(970) 349-2500   www.camp4coffee.com
Voted "Best Coffee in Colorado" by the Denver Post.

Paradise Café[H] - 303 Elk Avenue.
(970) 349-6233   Serving a good variety of breakfast and lunch foods.

The Secret Stash[I] - 21 Elk Avenue.
(970) 349-6245   www.thesecretstash.com
Dine in or take out, voted Crested Butte's best since 2002 (and good margs too!).

The Sunflower Deli[J] - 214 Elk Avenue.
(970) 349-6866   www.thesunflowerdeli.com
Fresh sandwiches, paninis, soups and salads, plus a great outdoor patio.

Teocali Tamale[K] - 311 ½ Elk Avenue.
(970) 349-2005   www.teocallitamale.com
An impressive selection of Mexican beers and affordable, fresh, healthy food to go with it.

Things to do in Bad Weather

Crested Butte Mountain Heritage Museum[L] - 331 Elk Avenue. (970) 349-1880
www.crestedbutteheritagemuseum.com
Bring quarters. Among other displays depicting activities that were a part of the regions' history, is a large train diorama with a train that takes trips through 1920 Crested Butte for only 25 cents. Skiing, mining and ranching exhibits are also on display. $3 for adults/children under 12 FREE.

Trailhead Discovery Museum[M] -
Outpost Building (at the base of the ski area).
(970) 349-7160   www.trailheadkids.org
This museum was founded by parents in the area who recognized a need for a place for their children to learn and play creatively, especially during the long winters. The exhibits include a dig pit, large play set, magnet table, art table, science station, painting easels and more. $

Crested Butte

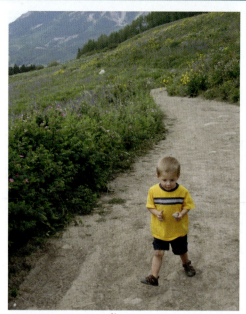

The Pottery Place^N - 502 Bellview Avenue. (970) 349-2799   www.crestedbuttestudio.com
For something a bit different, drop in to paint your own pottery! And, if you won't be in town long enough to see the piece fired, you can make arrangements with the studio for shipping. $

Groceries/Supplies

Clarks's Market^O - 500 Bellview Avenue. (970) 349-6492   www.clarksmarket.com

More Info

Old Rock Community Library^P - 507 Maroon Avenue. (970) 349-6535
www.gunnisoncountylibraries.org

Hospital/Emergency Care: *Gunnison Valley Hospital* - 711 North Taylor Street, Gunnison. (970) 641-1456   www.gvh-colorado.org

Crested Butte Medical Center - 214 Sixth Street (in the Ore Bucket Building). (970) 349-0321

Visitor Center & Chamber of Commerce^Q 601 Elk Avenue. (970) 349-6438 or (800) 545-4505 www.cbchamber.com

Additional information at: www.gunnisoncrestedbutte.com

Other Fun Stuff

Ski Lift^R (970) 349-2262 or (888) 317-6482 www.skicb.com   If the kids are old enough, take a ride on the Silver Queen or Red Lady Express. At the top enjoy the breathtaking views, have a picnic or take a hike. $

The Adventure Park (on Mt. Crested Butte)^S - (970) 349-2262   www.skicb.com
This new adventure park has a climbing wall, bungee trampolines and a mini-golf course (which is under the weather-protected tent!). $

Directions

The only paved road into Crested Butte is CO-135 from the south.

Parking

Plenty of free parking street side (try the side streets if the main ones are crowded).

Crested Butte

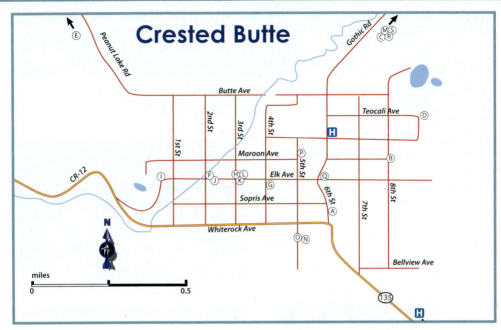

- A. Town Park – on 6th Street/CO-135
- B. Rainbow Park – Maroon & 8th
- C. Oh-Be-Joyful Picnic/Camping Area – 3.4 miles west on Slate River Rd; on the left
- D. Rec Path – east end of Teocali Avenue
- E. Peanut Lake/Lower Loop – 1.1 miles west of the end of town on Butte Avenue/Peanut Lake Rd.
- F. The Brick Oven – 223 Elk Avenue
- G. Camp 4 Coffee – 402 ½ Elk Avenue
- H. Paradise Café – 303 Elk Avenue
- I. The Secret Stash – 21 Elk Avenue
- J. The Sunflower Deli – 214 Elk Avenue
- K. Teocali Tamale – 311 ½ Elk Avenue
- L. CB Mountain Heritage Museum – 331 Elk Avenue
- M. Trailhead Discovery Museum – Outpost Building (at the base of the ski area)
- N. The Pottery Place – 502 Bellview Avenue
- O. Clark's Market – 500 Bellview Avenue
- P. Old Rock Community Library – 507 Maroon Ave
- Q. Visitor Center – 601 Elk Avenue
- R. Ski Lift – Mt. Crested Butte ski area
- S. The Adventure Park – Mt. Crested Butte ski area

photo by Nathan Pulley

Denver
"The Mile High City"

Like any metropolis, Denver is big. Never fear, it has loads of great family places to stop for a few minutes or a few hours, and they are easy to get to.

The Place to Go

Gates Crescent Park[A] - (Children's Museum Dr and 7th St) This park is a good pick because it's super easy to get to off the interstate, *and* there's parking at the *Children's Museum*.[H] Oh yes, and the kids will enjoy the playground (at the northern most end of the park). There are also picnic tables in the shade, the *Platte River Trail* for short walks, and a toilet.

Splash Spot

Confluence Park[C] - (Little Raven & 15th - limited street-side parking along both roads.) Big surprise, this park sits at the confluence of two rivers (Cherry Creek and the Platte River), and a stop here will require a dip in the water. You won't be alone, either, as it's a favorite spot among locals and kayakers. There are great places for picnics here, including tables with umbrellas. Unfortunately no restrooms. The *Platte River Trail* and the *Cherry Creek Trail* are both accessible from here.

Another Park

Downtown Children's Playground[B] - (Exit 212, take Speer, left on Wewatta, right on 15th and right again on Wynkoop.) There's limited street-side parking and a paid parking lot at the end of Wynkoop.)

Just off the *Cherry Creek Trail*, try the Downtown Children's Playground if you have a bit of time and are interested in being near downtown. Unfortunately, there are no restroom facilities. After some time on the playground, it's a short walk to the *16th Street Mall*.[P]

Trails for Strollers & Little Folks

Cherry Creek Trail - Within the city and county of Denver there are more than 80 miles of trails. The Cherry Creek Trail, 12.8 miles total, runs through the heart of Denver along Cherry Creek. Access at *Confluence Park*.[C]

South Platte River Trail - The trail follows the South Platte River for 12.5 miles. Access at *Confluence Park*[C] or *Gates Crescent*.[A]

Denver Parks:
www.denvergov.org/Parks

Kid-Friendly Eateries
(with something for adults too!)

El Señor Sol[D] - 2301 7th Street. (303) 455-2500 www.elsenorsol.com   Authentic (and yummy) Mexican food, plus easy parking.

Denver

The Old Spaghetti Factory [E] - 1215 18th
Street. (303) 295-1864 www.osf.com
Well, spaghetti. Lots of it in all shapes and sauces, including a gluten-free menu!

Proto's Pizza [F] - 2401 15th Street.
(720) 855-9400 www.protospizza.com
True Neapolitan pizza that continues to win praises from both local and national publications. Gluten-free pizzas available as well.

Wynkoop Brewing Company [G] - 1634 18th
Street. (303) 297-2700 www.wynkoop.com
An overwhelming menu of "goose-bump-inducing beers of moderate strength," and good food too!

Things to do in Bad Weather

Children's Museum of Denver [H] -
2121 Children's Museum Drive. (303) 433-7444
www.mychildsmuseum.org
Stop in to discover, explore and investigate the interactive Playscapes. The fun includes a fire station (with a real fire truck!), an assembly plant, a bubble room and other hands-on activities. $

Downtown Aquarium [I] - 700 Water Street.
(303) 561-4450 www.aquariumrestaurants.com/downtownaquariumdenver/default.asp
From the rainforest to coral lagoons to the oceans, the various water ecosystems are filled with amazing creatures. As you visit each exhibit you may find a sea turtle swimming above you or a shark lurking below. At the end, stop to feed the sting rays...really. $

Tattered Cover Bookstore [J] - 1628 16th
Street. (303) 436-1070 www.tatteredcover.com
This enormous, well-stocked book store will keep everyone busy for a while.

Groceries/Supplies

King Soopers[K] - 1331 Speer Boulevard
(303) 571-5566

Vitamin Cottage[L] - 2375 15th Street
(303) 458-5300

More Info

Denver Public Library[M] -
10 W 14th Avenue Pkwy . (720) 865-1111
http://denverlibrary.org/   Paid parking is available at the Cultural Center garage (12th & Broadway) for $1.00/hour, or at street-side meters.

Auraria Library[N] - *1100 Lawrence Street*
(303) 556-2639   http://library.auraria.edu/
Paid parking is available in the garage at 7th & Lawrence.

Hospital/Emergency Care: *Denver Health Medical Center -*
777 Bannock Street. (303) 436-6000
www.denverhealth.org

Convention & Visitors Bureau[O] -
VISIT DENVER's Visitor Information Center - 16th & California on the 16th Street Mall
(303) 892-1112   www.denver.org

Other Fun Stuff

16th Street Mall[P] - The mile-long pedestrian mall is lined with trees and flowers, restaurants and shops, but the kids will think that its best feature is the free shuttle bus to ride up and down the mall. They might also like the fountains and daily entertainers.

Platte Valley Trolley - (Denver Rail Heritage Society) *(303) 458-6255*   denvertrolley.org
Seasonal operation Friday-Sunday, noon-3pm. If you have 30 minutes, the kids will love a ride on an open trolley car along the South Platte. The operators are also very knowledgeable about the history of the trolley car and the area in which the car runs. Tickets are available at the *Children's Museum*[H] or *Aquarium*[I]. $

Denver

Directions
On I-25? Zero in on exits 211 and 212 for easy access to stops.

Parking
This may be tricky. There is metered parking all across downtown, as well as a few paid parking lots.

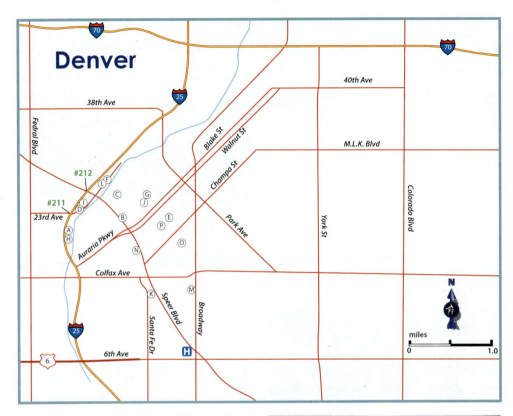

A. Gates Crescent Park – Children's Museum Drive & 7th Street
B. Downtown Children's Playground - Wewatta Street & Speer Blvd
C. Confluence Park – Little Raven St & 15th
D. El Senor Sol – 2301 7th Street
E. The Old Spaghetti Factory – 1215 18th Street
F. Proto's Pizza – 2401 15th Street
G. Wynkoop Brewing Company – 1634 18th Street
H. Children's Museum of Denver – 2121 Children's Museum Drive
I. Downtown Aquarium – 700 Water Street
J. Tattered Cover Bookstore – 1628 16th Street
K. King Soopers - 1331 Speer Blvd
L. Vitamin Cottage – 2375 15th Street
M. Denver Public Library – 10 W. 14th Ave Parkway
N. Auraria Library – 1100 Lawrence Street
O. Visitor Information Center – 16th & California on the 16th Street Mall
P. 16th Street Mall – 16th St b/n Market & Broadway

Dillon

Most people usually speak of this town as Dillon/Silverthorne, or simply zoom past on I-25. However, Dillon is its own unique town just a bit removed from the rest of the hustle and bustle of Summit County. If you venture a few miles off the interstate you'll find a quiet community, sitting above the picturesque Dillon Reservoir, with a lot to offer.

The Place to Go

Marina Park [A] - (Along Lodgepole St just west of the marina) Not only is the view overlooking Dillon Reservoir and the mountains spectacular, but this park is stocked with amenities. There is a great playground with many different pieces of equipment, a sand box, covered picnic tables, public restrooms and access to the trail that runs along the side of the reservoir.

Splash Spot

Dillon Reservoir - Swimming is prohibited in the reservoir, however, kerplunking a few rocks and floating a few sticks is not. Either go to the *Dillon Marina*[L], or walk down the paths at *Marina Park*[A].

Trails for Strollers & Little Folks

Dillon Bike Path - This paved bike path could take you all over Summit County if you were so inclined. It also loops (partly on Swan Mountain Rd) all the way around Dillon Reservoir.

Kid-Friendly Eateries
(with something for adults too!)

Arapahoe Café & Pub [C] -
626 Lake Dillon Drive. (970) 468-0873
www.arapahoecafe.com
In Summit County since 1945, this restaurant (serving breakfast, lunch and dinner) keeps racking up awards for its brunch and barbeque, plus there's a great patio.

Another Park

Dillon Town Park [B] - (On Buffalo St) If Marina Park isn't enough for the kids, try Dillon Town Park. There is another playground, a covered pavilion, picnic tables, a wide open field for expending energy, and public restrooms.

Dam Brewery [D] - 100 Little Dam Street.
(970) 262-7777   www.dambrewery.com
As they say, "Dam good beer" (and, of course, good food to go with it).

Dillon 47

Kula's Café and Coffee Shop[E] -
119 La Bonte Street. (970) 513-8336
Gluten free options and award winning soup. And yes, coffee.

Things to do in Bad Weather

Summit Historical Society: Dillon Schoolhouse[F] - 403 La Bonte Street.
(970) 468-2207   The schoolhouse was built in 1883, converted to a church in 1910, then into a museum in 1972. Today it is full of turn-of-the-century artifacts, including desks, readers, slates, a Centennial flag, globes, a phonograph and more. $

Silverthorne Recreation Center[G] -
430 Rainbow Drive, Silverthorne. (970) 262-7370
Yes, drive to Silverthorne (it's not far). The recreation center is a gem. The swimming area has four pools and three water slides, and temperatures range from 90-92°. Visitors can also play in the gym, run on the track, drop in on a fitness class or use the weight room. $

Groceries/Supplies

Natural Grocers[H] - 761 Anemone Trail. (970) 262-1100

City Market[I] - 300 Dillon Ridge Road. (970) 468-2363

More Info

Summit County Library: North Branch[J]
651 Center Circle, Silverthorne. (970) 468-5887
www.co.summit.co.us/library

Hospital/Emergency Care:
St. Anthony's Summit Medical Center -
340 Peak 1 Drive, Frisco. (970) 668-3300
www.summitmedicalcenter.org

High Country Health Care -
265 Tanglewood Lane, Suite E-1, Silverthorne.
(970) 468-1003   www.highcountryhealth.com

Visitor's Center: Summit Information Center[K] - 246 Rainbow Drive (in Green Village).
(970) 468-5780

Town Information: www.townofdillon.com

Other Fun Stuff

Dillon Marina[L] - 300 Marina Drive.
(970) 468-5100   www.dillonmarina.com
The Dillon Marina is a full-service marina on the Dillon Reservoir. BYOB (boat, that is), or rent one, for a day on the water. Explore the lake, fish, or just bask in the sun.

Directions

From I-70, use exit 205.

Coming from the north on CO-9, continue under the I-70 overpass into town.

From Keystone or A-Basin, US-6 will bring you directly into town.

Dillon

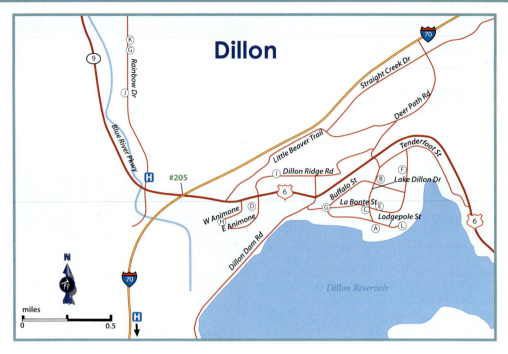

A. Marina Park – Along Lodgepole Street, just west of the marina
B. Dillon Town Park - located behind Town Hall and the Summit Historical Museum on Buffalo Street
C. Arapahoe Café & Pub – 626 Lake Dillon Drive
D. Dam Brewery – 100 Little Dam Street
E. Kula's Café and Coffee Shop – 119 LaBonte St
F. Dillon Schoolhouse – 403 LaBonte Street
G. Silverthorne Recreation Center – 430 Rainbow Drive, Silverthorne
H. Natural Grocers – 761 Anemone Trail
I. City Market – 300 Dillon Ridge Road
J. Summit County Library – North Branch – 651 Center Circle, Silverthorne
K. Visitor Center – 246 Rainbow Drive, Silverthorne
L. Dillon Marina – 300 Marina Drive

Durango

In the southwest corner of Colorado, almost where the Rockies meet the desert, is Durango. It sits in the Animas River Valley, with the river flowing through it, surrounded by millions of acres of national forest land.

The Place to Go

Downtown[A] - The historic downtown area of Durango is the best spot for a little of everything. The quintessential Main Street is a Nationally Registered Historic District and is full of hotels, restaurants, brewpubs, art galleries, museums and shops.

Trolley Rides – And for the kids, take a trolley ride! It stops along Main Avenue every 20 minutes, and runs through downtown. $

Buckley Park[B] - (Main and 12th St) At the northernmost end of Main Avenue, this park has grass, shade and rocks to climb.

Parking: Metered street-side parking mostly. Municipal lots available after hours and on weekends along Camino del Rio, and at Main Avenue and 5th Street.

Parks

Fassbinder Park[C] - (17th St and W 2nd Ave) This small park is a lovely place to stop and lay in the grass. There's also loads of shade, picnic tables, a playground and public restrooms.

Santa Rita Park[D] - (149 S Camino del Rio) For those that want a stop without going downtown, this is the place. By the Animas River, this park has water access, fishing areas, the *Animas River Trail*, picnic tables, a great playground, a restroom (at the north end of the park) and picnic shelters. Best of all, there's easy parking, and the visitor center is there.

Splash Spot

Animas River - The river runs through town, offering many opportunities to dip toes or to toss a few rocks. Try *Schneider Park*,[E] or stroll along the *Animas River Trail* until you find a nice spot.

Trails for Strollers & Little Folks

Animas River Trail - This hard-surface trail runs along the river for almost seven miles through town. There are multiple access points, including *Santa Rita Park*,[D] *Schneider Park*,[E] *the Rec Center*[N] and across the river from *City Market North*.[P]

Colorado Trail & Junction Creek[F] - While not recommended for strollers, this trail allows hikers to experience part of the 469-mile Colorado Trail. For kids, it's a chance to explore the woods while everyone enjoys the views.

Horse Gulch [G] - For a quick hike right from town, try Horse Gulch. The natural surface trail system has over 50 miles of trails. No strollers.

Kid-Friendly Eateries
(with something for adults too!)

Brickhouse Café & Coffee Bar [H] -
1849 Main Avenue. (970) 247-3760
www.brickhousecafe.com   Purportedly the best breakfast in town, served all day long.

Carver Brewing Company [I] -
1022 Main Avenue. (970) 259-2545
www.carverbrewing.com   Award-winning beer and fresh food. What more could you ask for?

Steaming Bean Coffee Company [J] -
915 Main Avenue. (970) 385-7901
http://www.thebean.com/store_durango.aspx
They serve a wide variety of food and gourmet coffee, plus there's a Kid's Corner with toys, games, and kid-sized tables and chairs.

Steamworks Brewing Company [K] -
801 E. 2nd Avenue. (970) 259-9200
http://www.steamworksbrewing.com/
Not only does this brewpub have beers that win awards at the Great American Brew Festival, it has an extensive pub menu.

Zia Taqueria [L] - 3101 Main Avenue.
(970) 247-3355   www.ziataqueria.com
Serving a "fresh-Mex menu," this restaurant has simple, authentic, affordable meals.

Things to do in Bad Weather

Durango Discovery Museum [M] -
1333 Camino del Rio (in the historic Powerhouse). (970) 259-9234   www.durangodiscovery.org
Their mission is to spark curiosity, ignite imagination and power exploration. The exhibits change regularly, but all are interactive and kid friendly, designed to teach visitors about energy past, present and future. $

Durango Community Recreation Center [N]
2700 Main Avenue. (970) 375-7300
www.durangogov.org/reccenter
Kids and their adults can spend the day playing in the rec center's indoor water park, whooshing down the giant water slide, floating on the lazy river, playing in the game room, climbing on the rock wall, and more. $

Trimble Hot Springs [O] - 6475 C.R. 203.
(970) 247-0111   www.trimblehotsprings.com
Located just five miles north of Durango on US-550, Trimble Hot Springs offers mineral-rich hot pools, a large swimming pool (temperatures ranging from 101-110°), and a great lawn for picnics and lounging. They also offer massages and spa treatments. $

Groceries/Supplies

City Market North [P] - 3130 Main Avenue.
(970) 259-0240

City Market [Q] - 6 Town Plaza. (970) 247-4475

Natural Grocers [R] - 1123 Camino Del Rio.
(970) 247-4100

More Info

Durango Public Library [S] -
1900 E. 3rd Avenue. (970) 375-3380
www.durangopubliclibrary.org

Hospital/Emergency Care: **Mercy Regional Medical Center** - 1010 Three Springs Boulevard. (970) 247-4311
www.mercydurango.org

Durango Urgent Care - 2577 N. Main Avenue. (970) 247-8382
www.durangourgentcare.com

Durango Area Tourism Office [T] -
111 S, Camino del Rio. (970) 247-3500 or (800) 525-8855   www.durango.org

Other Fun Stuff

D&S Narrow Gauge Railroad and Museum [U] - 479 Main Avenue (at the train station). (970) 247-2733 or (888) TRAIN-07
www.durangotrain.com
Kids will love it! They can see the roundhouse turntable in action when the trains return from Silverton in the evening. There are also historical exhibits. FREE

If you want to make a full day of it, jump on the Durango & Silverton Narrow Gauge Railroad train to Silverton. The historic train has been in continuous operation for over 125 years. The trip is 45 miles long and 3 ½ hours each way. $

Durango 51

Mesa Verde National Park[V] - *56 miles west of Durango on US-160. (970) 529-4465*
www.nps.gov/meve   This park is one of the most unique in our vast national park system. It protects over 4,000 archaeological sites, including 600 cliff dwellings of the Ancestral Pueblo people who lived in the area between 600-1300 AD. $

Directions

Durango lies at the intersection of US-550 and US-160.

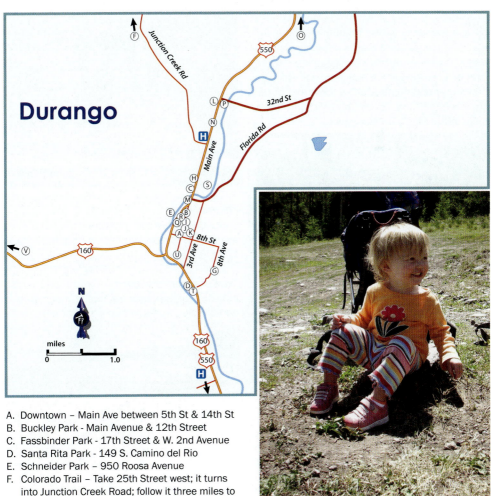

A. Downtown – Main Ave between 5th St & 14th St
B. Buckley Park - Main Avenue & 12th Street
C. Fassbinder Park - 17th Street & W. 2nd Avenue
D. Santa Rita Park - 149 S. Camino del Rio
E. Schneider Park – 950 Roosa Avenue
F. Colorado Trail – Take 25th Street west; it turns into Junction Creek Road; follow it three miles to parking on left, after entering the San Juan N.F.
G. Horse Gulch - 3rd St. and 9th Ave
H. Brickhouse Café & Coffee Bar – 1849 Main Ave
I. Carver Brewing Company – 1022 Main Avenue
J. Steaming Bean Coffee Company – 915 Main Ave
K. Steamworks Brewing Company – 801 E. 2nd Ave
L. Zia Taqueria – 3101 Main Avenue
M. Discovery Museum – 1333 Camino del Rio
N. Durango Rec Center – 2700 Main Ave
O. Trimble Hot Springs - 6475 C.R. 203
P. City Market North – 3130 Main Avenue
Q. City Market – 6 Town Plaza
R. Natural Grocers – 1123 Camino del Rio
S. Durango Public Library - 1900 E. 3rd Avenue
T. Durango Tourism Office – 111 S. Camino del Rio
U. D&S Narrow Gauge Railroad – 479 Main Avenue
V. Mesa Verde National Park – 56 miles west of Durango on US-160

Estes Park

Estes Park is literally the gateway to Rocky Mountain National Park. With a backdrop of towering mountains, Estes is a great family spot for all sorts of outdoor adventures and in-town activities.

The Place to Go

Downtown[A] - It's all in the downtown area: a playground, food, public restrooms, shopping, the *Riverwalk*, and even places to cool little feet in the river. There's a playground along the river at E. Riverside Drive (where you will also find public restrooms). Across the street at the *Riverside Plaza*[B] is where you'll want to dip a toe in the Big Thompson River.

Park

Stanley Park[C] - (on Community Drive) If you simply need a quick stop for run-around time and want to avoid downtown, try Stanley Park, which has a nice playground and is easy to get to. You can also access the *Lake Estes Trail loop* from here.

Splash Spot

Lake Estes Marina[D] - 1770 Big Thompson Rd (970) 586-2011
www.estesvalleyrecreation.com/marina.html
Aside from *Riverside Plaza*[B], the best place to go is the marina, located on the southeast side of Lake Estes, off US-34/Big Thompson Avenue. There's a sandy "beach" and picnic tables, a playground, restrooms, boat rentals and bicycle rentals (with child carriers!).

Trails for Strollers & Little Folks

Lake Estes Trail - This loop circles the lake (3.8 miles total), and offers fantastic views of Rocky Mountain. Be on the lookout for elk, especially in the spring and fall. Access at *Lake Estes Marina*[D] or the *Visitors Center*[L].

Riverwalk - The paved Riverwalk downtown is another option for a leisurely stroll, with the option to stop for treats along the way. Access at *Riverside Plaza*[B].

photos by Nathan Pulley

Estes Park

Kid-Friendly Eateries
(with something for adults too!)

DeLeo's Park Theatre Café & Deli [E] - 132 Moraine Ave (970) 577-1134
www.deleosdeli.com Stroll the length of the *Riverwalk* to the west end for the best Italian deli sandwiches and friendly service.

photos by Nathan Pulley

Laura's Fine Candies [F] - 129 Elkhorn Avenue. (970) 586-4004 www.laurasfudgeofestes.com
Oh, come on…sweet treats for everyone!

Ed's Cantina [G] - 390 East Elkhorn Avenue (970) 586-2919 www.edscantina.com
A variety of Mexican and American fare, a dedicated gluten-free menu, and great margaritas!

Kind Coffee [H] - 470 East Elkhorn Avenue (970) 586-5206 A locally owned coffee shop with parking right out front.

Things to do in Bad Weather

Estes Valley Library [I] - 335 E. Elkhorn Ave (970) 586-8116 www.estesvalleylibrary.org
Besides books, the youth room has a neat train table, thanks to a donation from the Estes Valley Model Railroaders.

Estes Park Aquatic Center [J] - 660 Community Dr. (970) 586-2340
www.estesvalleyrecreation.com/aquatic.html
Visitors here are welcome to enjoy the wading pool, rope swing, lap swimming and more. $

Groceries/Supplies

Safeway [K] - 451 E Wonderview Avenue. (970) 586-4447   In the Stanley Village center, near the intersection of US-34 and US-36.

More Info

Hospital/Emergency Care: *Estes Park Medical Center* - 555 Prospect Ave (970) 586-2317   www.epmedcenter.com

Estes Park Visitor's Center [L]
500 Big Thompson Avenue (970) 577-9900 or (800) 44-ESTES   www.estesparkcvb.com

Other Fun Stuff

Estes Park Ride-A-Kart [M] -
2250 Big Thompson Avenue (970) 586-6495
www.rideakart.com   This family amusement park, in operation for over 50 years, has a little something for everyone. Key attractions include a miniature train, bumper boats, bumper cars, miniature golf, and race cars. $

Rocky Mountain National Park [N] -
(970) 586-1206   www.nps.gov/romo
www.rockymountainnationalpark.com
With its glowing meadows and jagged peaks, Rocky Mountain is a national treasure. Wildlife thrives in the park, allowing visitors numerous opportunities to listen to elk bugle or watch critters scurry across rocks (watch out for rogue chipmunks…they'll steal your sandwich!). There are countless trails, but for a hike with kids try the Sprague Lake trail. $

Estes Park Aerial Tramway [O] -
420 E. Riverside Drive (970) 586-3675
www.estestram.com
Kids love trams, and you'll love the scenery. Opened in 1955, this tramway offers visitors a ride to the top of Prospect Mountain for stunning views of the mountains and Estes Park. $

Estes Park

Directions

From the west, take Trail Ridge Road through the park; stay on US-36 heading east; this will take you to Elkhorn Avenue, the main street downtown.

From the east, take US-36 or US 34 west, past Lake Estes. Follow signs to downtown, which will lead you down Elkhorn Avenue.

From the south, follow CO-7 until it meets US-36. To get downtown, turn left onto US-36/North St. Vrain Avenue and left again onto Elkhorn Avenue.

Parking

There are numerous public parking lots downtown, including one on Elkhorn Avenue by the library, and one on Moraine Avenue (at the west end of downtown).

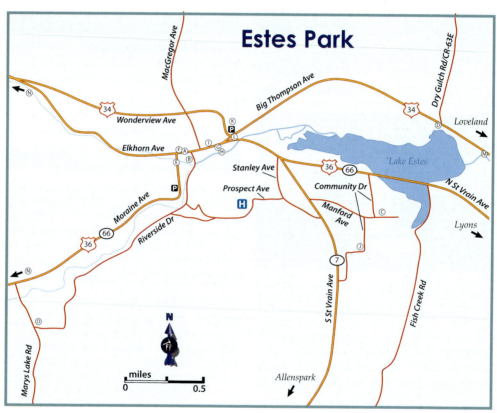

A. Downtown
B. Riverside Plaza (on the west side of Riverside Drive and the river)
C. Stanley Park (south from US-36 on Community Dr, near the Fairgrounds)
D. Lake Estes Marina - 1770 Big Thompson Rd
E. DeLeo's Park Theatre Café and Deli - 132 Moraine Ave (west end of downtown)
F. Laura's Fine Candies - 129 Elkhorn Avenue
G. Ed's Cantina - 390 East Elkhorn Avenue
H. Kind Coffee - 470 East Elkhorn Avenue
I. Estes Valley Library - 335 E. Elkhorn Ave
J. Aquatic Center - 660 Community Dr
K. Safeway - 451 E. Wonderview Avenue
L. Estes Park Vistor's Center - intersection of US-36 and US-34
M. Estes Ride-A-Kart - 2250 Big Thompson Ave
N. Rocky Mountain National Park (multiple entry points)
O. Aerial Tramway - 420 E. Riverside Dr

Fairplay

"Trout fishing capital of Colorado"

Surrounded by the Mosquito and Park mountain ranges, Fairplay lies in a broad valley that covers over 900 square miles. The nearby South Platte River and its many forks make Fairplay a mecca for fishermen (and women).

The Place to Go

Cohen Park[A] - (8th and Bogue St) Cohen Park is a hidden gem. Just a few blocks off the main road, it has swings, slides, a covered picnic area, restrooms and three different play areas (one for younger children, two for older ones).

Another Park

Alma Playground & Park[B] - (E. Buckskin Road, Alma) www.townofalma.com
Located five miles up the road, Alma has a surprisingly nice spot to stop with kids. This itty-bitty town (the highest incorporated town in North America at 10,578 feet) could easily be overlooked, but it can boast one of the nicest quiet stops in Colorado.

At the park there is not only a great playground, but also shaded picnic tables and restrooms. The best part, though, is its "beach." The small, sandy spot is ideal for wading and playing.

Splash Spots

Fairplay Beach[C] - Along the South Platte River which borders town, Fairplay Beach is a favorite fishing spot. You'll also find a stage (concerts are held here throughout the summer), campsites, grills and restrooms.

Alma[B] - Along the banks of the South Platte River, Alma has a wonderful sandy wading area at the park. The sandy, gentle slope into the river is the perfect spot for kids to play the water.

Kid-Friendly Eateries
(with something for adults too!)

Alma Natural Food & Coffee House[D] - 131 N. Main Street, Alma. (719) 836-4847
Half coffee house (upstairs) and half natural food store (downstairs), this place is known for its great food and great coffee.

Beary, Beary Tastee Bakery[E] - 600 Main Street. (719) 836-3212
www.bearybearytastee.com
The bakery serves a full German menu, a lunch menu, and more. If that's not enough, enjoy an award-winning baked treat or some of the World Famous Rocky Mountain Granola.

Java Moose[F] - 730 Main Street. (719) 836-0770
Espresso, pastries, burritos, salads and gourmet sandwiches for breakfast and lunch.

Silver Scoop Creamery[G] - 456 Front Street. (719) 836-3403 www.silverscoopcreamery.com
Step back in time at this classic soda and ice cream parlor.

Things to do in Bad Weather

South Park Recreation Center[H] - 1190 Bullet Road. (719) 836-0747
www.southparkrec.org
Stop in to splash in the leisure play area accented with palm trees and sprayers. You'll feel like you're in the tropics. $

Fairplay

Groceries/Supplies

Prather's Market[I] - 301 US-285.
(719) 836-1618

More Info

Fairplay Library[J] - 418 Main Street.
(719) 836-4297 www.parkcounty.colibraries.org
Not only is the library housed in a historic building, but there's also a wide open grassy area out front, as well as a gazebo.

Hospital/Emergency Care: *Timberline Clinic* - 980 Main Street. (719) 836-3455

Southpark Medical Group - 525 Hathaway.
(719) 836-1900   www.southparkmedicalgroup.com

South Park Chamber of Commerce[K] -
417 Front Street. (719) 836-3410
www.realfairplay.com

Other Fun Stuff

Front Street[L] - Really, Fairplay has a downtown! This quaint mountain town has a thriving business community and vibrant local arts. Take a stroll down Front Street to visit the majority of businesses in Fairplay.

South Park City[M] - 100 4th Street.
(719) 836-2387   www.southparkcity.org
South Park City is an accurate recreation of a frontier mining town between 1860 and 1900. It is home to 34 authentic buildings, each housing artifacts of the time period. A visit is like a walk through time to the old west. $

Directions

Fairplay sits at the intersection of US-285 and CO-9.

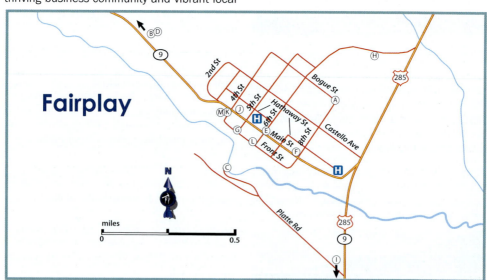

A. Cohen Park – 8th & Bogue Street
B. Alma Playground & Park – E. Buckskin Rd., Alma
C. Fairplay Beach – From CO-9/US-285 south of town, turn onto Platte Dr; follow about 0.5mi to Beach Rd
D. Alma Natural Food and Coffeehouse – 131 N. Main St, Alma
E. Beary, Beary Tastee Bakery – 600 Main Street
F. Java Moose – 730 Main Street
G. Silver Scoop Creamery – 456 Front Street
H. South Park Recreation Center – 1190 Bullet Rd
I. Prather's Market – 301 US-285
J. Fairplay Library – 418 Main Street
K. South Park Chamber of Commerce – 417 Front St
L. Front Street – Front St, between 4th and 8th St
M. South Park City – 100 4th Street

Fort Collins

Once you visit, you'll understand why it continues to be nationally ranked as an outstanding town for families.

The Place to Go

City Park[A] - (1500 W. Mulberry St) Go to City Park. You'll probably find that it ends up being more than just a short stop, though, because there's so much to do...so be prepared. From Mulberry Street turn onto Sheldon Drive and follow that road as it meanders through the old shade trees to Sheldon Lake. Enjoy paddle boat rentals, *City Park Pool*, a large playground, *City Park Railway*[B], picnic tables and loads of places to simply relax in the grass.

City Park Railway[B] - (in City Park) (970) 221-6337   If you go to City Park, you'll have to ride the miniature train. As it laps around the short course it passes through a tunnel and the conductor blows the train whistle...every kid's dream. $

Other Parks

Lee Martinez Park[C] - (600 N Sherwood St) A smaller, alternative park is Lee Martinez. From Cherry Street head north onto N. Sherwood. Parking for the park and playground is to the right. There's also a picnic shelter, restrooms and access to the *Poudre River Trail*.

The Farm at Lee Martinez Park[D] - (600 N Sherwood St) (970) 221-6665
www.fcgov.com/thefarm   If there's time, visit the farm at the park. For a small entrance fee kids can watch, pet and feed a variety of farm animals. There's also a small museum about farm life, as well as the history of farming and agriculture in the community. $

Library Park[E] - (207 Peterson St) Library Park is a good choice if you're already downtown and need a playground but don't want to get in the car again. In adddition to a playground, you'll find the *Fort Collins Museum and Discovery Science Center*[N] and the *Main Library*[Q] there.

Fossil Creek Park[F] - (5821 S. Lemay Ave) If the kids love dinosaurs, and you don't want to be near downtown, this is a good stop. Not only is there a giant wooly mammoth to climb, but there are "fossils" embedded in the walls. Kids can also climb the rock wall or play on one of several playground structures. Closer to Portner Reservoir there's "Adventure Island" and an interactive water feature, as well as a walking trail.

Splash Spots

Oak Street Plaza Park ^G - (At Oak St and College Ave) The interactive fountains here are loads of fun for the kids and quite entertaining to watch. It's a great place for a quick cool down.

City Park Pool - 1599 City Park Drive (970) 484-7665   www.fcgov.com/recreation/cityparkpoolandtrain.php   This outdoor pool, located in *City Park*, ^A includes a 30-foot drop slide, a curly slide, a lazy river, geysers and a large play structure. $

Trails for Strollers & Little Folks

Trails Map - www.fcgov.com/parks/pdf/trailmap.pdf

Poudre River Trail - The Poudre River Trail runs, well, along the Poudre River (for 10 miles). It's great for hiking and biking, or just wandering and picking up sticks and leaves. Easy access is found from *Lee Martinez Park*; ^C and if you start here it's only a short walk northwest to the Salyer Natural Area.

Riverbend Ponds Natural Area ^H - (Follow Mulberry east from downtown) www.fcgov.com/naturalareas/finder/riverbend Riverbend Ponds is one of dozens of "natural areas" in Fort Collins. Here you'll find three miles of trails through wetlands, by ponds, and along the Poudre River. There's also a self-guided interpretive trail. The area is home to over 200 species of birds, so keep your eyes open.

Kid-Friendly Eateries
(with something for adults too!)

Ben and Jerry's ^I - 1 Old Town Square. (970) 407-0899   www.benandjerrys.com
Premium ice cream, sorbet and frozen yogurt. Yum.

Big City Burrito ^J - 510 South College Avenue (970) 482-3303   www.bigcityburrito.com
Their mission: "You walk in hungry. You walk out happy. Mission accomplished."

Fort Collins

CooperSmith's Pub and Brewing [K] -
5 Old Town Square. (970) 498-0483
www.coopersmithspub.com
Sandwiches, pub food and BEER!

Pickle Barrel [L] - 122 W. Laurel Street.
(970) 484-0235 So many sandwiches to choose from (and they're all good)!

There are many other *fast food* and dine-in options available, especially along US-287, south of downtown.

Things to do in Bad Weather

The Children's Play Area at the Foothills Mall [M] - 215 East Foothills Parkway (near Macy's). (970) 226-5556
A good rainy-day activity. The 2,200 square foot play area is great for climbing and burning off energy. FREE

Fort Collins Museum and Discovery Science Center [N] - 200 Mathews Street.
(970) 221-6738 fcmdsc.org
The partnership between the Fort Collins Museum and the Discovery Science Center combines hands-on science exhibits with cultural displays to spark imagination and curiosity in visitors young and old. $

Groceries/Supplies

Safeway [O] - 460 S. College Ave. (970) 484-0222

Whole Foods [P] - 2201 College. (970) 267-9200

More Info

Main Library [Q] - 201 Peterson Street (at Library Park). (970) 221-6680 – Children's Services   www.poudrelibraries.org

Hospital/Emergency Care: *Poudre Valley Hospital* - 1024 S. Lemay Avenue.
(970) 495-7000   www.pvhs.org

Fort Collins Convention and Visitors Bureau [R] - 19 Old Town Square. (970) 232-3840 or (800) 274-3218   visitftcollins.com

More info: ftcollins.com

Other Fun Stuff

Horsetooth Reservoir [S] - (Follow Harmony Rd. west from downtown)
(970) 223-0140 – Inlet Bay Marina
www.co.larimer.co.us/parks/horsetooth.htm
This open space is in the foothills west of Fort Collins. There are many trails here, as well as a variety of water-sport opportunities, including swimming at South Bay. Other amenities available. $

Lory State Park [T] - 708 Lodgepole Dr, Bellvue.
(970) 493-1623   parks.state.co.us/parks/lory/Pages/LoryStatePark.aspx   In the park there are 20 miles of trails to choose from, and most are great for little hikers (not much elevation gain). You'll also find picnic areas, a visitor center and restrooms. $

Fort Fun [U] - 1513 East Mulberry Street.
(970) 472-8000   www.fortfun.biz
Fort Fun is a 14-acre indoor and outdoor fun park. Activities include Go-Karts, mini-golf, laser tag, a giant slide, bumper cars, the Adventure Train and much, much more. $

Directions

From I-25 exit 269; follow CO-14/East Mulberry St west; it will intersect US-287/College Ave.

From the north or south, follow US-287/College Avenue through town.

Fort Collins

A. City Park - 1500 W. Mulberry Street
B. City Park Railway – 1599 City Park Drive
C. Lee Martinez Park - 600 N. Sherwood Street
D. The Farm at Lee Martinez Park – 600 N. Sherwood Street
E. Library Park – 207 Peterson Street
F. Fossil Creek Park – 5821 S. Lemay Avenue (From S. College Ave/US-287, follow Fossil Creek Parkway east to S. Lemay Ave. Turn left. The park will be on the left.)
G. Oak Street Plaza Park – at Oak St and College Ave
H. Riverbend Ponds Natural Area - Parking lots on Cherly St (off Summitview), Prospect St, Cairnes St (off Timberline).
I. Ben & Jerry's – 1 Old Town Square
J. Big City Burrito – 510 S. College Avenue
K. CooperSmith's Pub – 5 Old Town Square
L. Pickle Barrel – 122 W. Laurel Street
M. Foothills Mall – 215 E. Foothills Parkway
N. Fort Collins Museum & Discovery Science Center – 200 Mathews Street
O. Safeway – 460 S. College Avenue
P. Whole Foods – 2201 S. College Avenue
Q. Main Library – 201 Peterson Street
R. Fort Collins Convention and Visitors Bureau – 19 Old Town Square
S. Horsetooth Reservoir – from US-287 take Harmony Road west
T. Lory State Park – 708 Lodgepole Drive, Bellvue
U. Fort Fun – 1513 E. Mulberry Street

Fort Morgan

The original fort was built by the federal government in 1864-65 to protect the mail service and immigrants along the Overland Trail. Its pioneer spirit prevailed, and today Fort Morgan is a thriving plains community approximately 80 miles west of Denver.

The Place to Go

Riverside Park[A] - (1600 Main St) Surprise! Most folks zoom past Fort Morgan, or pull into one of the many fast food parking lots. But this beautiful, large city park should not be missed. Not only does it have a playground, but also shaded lawns, picnic tables, horseshoe pits, and restrooms. In addition, the park offers free overnight camping and has an outdoor swimming pool.

photos by Nathan Pulley

Another Park

City Park[B] - (414 Main St) If you're looking for "one-stop stopping" this is it. Located in downtown on Main Street, City Park has a playground, picnic tables, restrooms and a train to climb on. The library and museum are also here, as well as places to eat nearby.

Splash Spot

Riverside Park Pool - After playing in *Riverside Park*[A] or going for a walk, stop at the outdoor pool for a little splash time. $

Trails for Strollers & Little Folks

Riverside Park[A] - Within the park there are numerous options for different length "hikes" with no elevation gain. You can also walk along the South Platte River at the southern end of the park.

Kid-Friendly Eateries
(with something for adults too!)

Cables' Pub and Grill[C] - 431 Main Street. (970) 867-6144   www.cablespubandgrill.com
"Where friends meet." Serving sandwiches, burgers, drinks and even food for the kids!

Café Lotus[D] - 307 East Kiowa Avenue. (970) 542-0800   www.cafe-lotus.com
Light breakfast, a great sandwich selection for lunch, coffee drinks and a kids' area with toys and plush chairs.

Arby's (with drive-thru)[E] - 1218 North Main Street. (970) 867-6888

Peppy Coffee[F] - 1002 Main Street. (970) 867-7800   Strictly a drive-thru, but if you need coffee, you need coffee.

Things to do in Bad Weather

Fort Morgan Museum[G] - 414 Main Street. (970) 542-4010   www.ftmorganmus.org
Use a "Guide to the Gallery" to tour this museum and learn about irrigation along the South Platte River Valley, Fort Morgan as a military encampment, ranching in the county, Native American history and more. Kids "discovery hunts" are also available. FREE

62 Fort Morgan

Groceries/Supplies

Safeway[H] - 620 W. Platte Avenue. (970) 867-3377

More Info

Fort Morgan Public Library[I] - 414 Main Street. (970) 542-4000 The library is located in the same building as the museum at *City Park*[B]. The whole downstairs area is dedicated to children.

Hospital/Emergency Care: *Colorado Plains Medical Center* - 1000 Lincoln St. (970) 867-3391 coloradoplainsmedicalcenter.com

Fort Morgan Area Chamber of Commerce[J] - 300 Main Street. (970) 867-6702 or (800) 354-8660   www.fortmorganchamber.org

Other Fun Stuff

Jackson Lake State Park[K] - (Follow CO-144 west for approximately 20 miles) (970) 645-2551   They call this park "an oasis on the plains" with good reason. It has been named one of the top 15 park beaches by Reserve America (and the shallow water warms quickly in the summer!). The park also has great boating opportunities, fishing, and the half-mile Prairie Wetlands Nature Trail and other trails. $

Shoreline Marina[L] - (970) 645-2628 http://shorelinemarina.biz   This marina at *Jackson Lake*[K] is fully stocked with everything you might need for fishing, camping and boating. It's also the place to go if you'd like to rent a boat (pontoons, fishing boats and jet-skis). $

Directions

From I-76, exit 80 (CO-52); drive north to Riverside Park, or south to town (CO-52 turns into Main Street)

A. Riverside Park – 1600 Main St, just north of the interstate
B. City Park – 414 Main Street
C. Cables' Pub and Grill – 431 Main Street
D. Café Lotus – 307 East Kiowa Avenue
E. Arby's – 1218 North Main Street
F. Peppy Coffee – 1002 Main Street
G. Fort Morgan Museum – 414 Main Street
H. Safeway – 620 W. Platte
I. Fort Morgan Public Library – 414 Main Street
J. Ft Morgan Chamber of Commerce – 300 Main St
K. Jackson Lake State Park – 26363 CR-3, Orchard
L. Shoreline Marina – Jackson Lake State Park – 26363 County Road 3, Orchard, CO

Frisco

"Main Street to the Rockies"

Frisco is at the heart of Summit County, on the shores of Dillon Reservoir and surrounded by towering peaks. And small though it may be, it is full of charm, adventure, and endless choices for outdoor activities.

The Place to Go

Marina Park[A] - (900 Main St, on the reservoir) Easy to get to, either from the interstate, or CO-9, Marina Park has a great little playground, stunning views, lots of parking, and public restrooms. There's also access to the bike path for a stroll by the water.

Other Parks

Walter Byron Memorial Park[B] - (306 Creekside Drive) For a secluded rest and play stop, this park is a great bet. Not only is there a playground, but also covered picnic tables, open fields, fishing, rec path access and restrooms. Better still, it's on *Ten Mile Creek*[D] so kids can splash in the water.

Meadow Creek Park[C] - (828 Meadow Dr) This small park sits on Meadow Creek Pond, and has a playground, picnic tables, fishing, and access to bike paths. A portable toilet is available in the summer.

Splash Spot

Ten Mile Creek[D] - On a hot day nothing beats wading into a cool creek. On not-so-hot days the kids can also entertain themselves by throwing rocks into the water or floating sticks downstream. Access at *Walter Byron Memorial Park*.[B]

Trails for Strollers & Little Folks

Rec Path - Within the town limits, there are 12 miles of paved paths, and these paths connect to the Summit County Recreational Pathway System (which connects towns and resorts across Summit County). Try taking the Lakefront Rec Path north from the marina. This takes you along the shore of Dillon Reservoir.

Willow Preserve[E] - This short, boardwalk path has a nature trail (with interpretive signs) and overlooks.

Rainbow Lake[F] - Rainbow Lake is a great little hike that starts right in town. It isn't recommended for strollers, but the small hikers will enjoy the walk in the woods with little elevation gain.

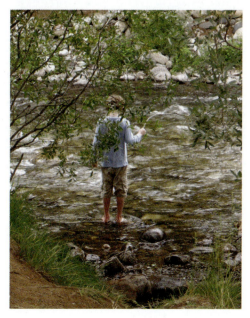

Kid-Friendly Eateries
(with something for adults too!)

Abbey's Coffee[G] - 720 Main St. (970) 668-8710
Friendly local shop with excellent coffee.

Backcountry Brewery[H] - 720 Main Street (970) 668-2337   www.backcountrybrewery.com
"Great brews. Great views. Great food."

Butterhorn Bakery and Café[I] - 408 Main Street. (970) 668-3997
www.butterhornbakery.com
A Summit County favorite among locals and returning visitors, this place serves homemade, affordable food for breakfast and lunch.

Deli Belly's[J] - 275 Main Street. (970) 668-9255
Simple, quick and delicious deli sandwiches.

The Island Grill[K] - 900 Main Street. (970) 668-9999   A full-service restaurant right at the marina, open seasonally.

Log Cabin Café[L] - 121 Main St. (970) 668-3947
www.log-cabin-cafe.com   Serving an extensive breakfast and lunch menu, there's sure to be something for everyone.

Things to do in Bad Weather

Frisco Historic Park & Museum[M] - 120 Main Street. (970) 668-3428
www.townoffrisco.com/activities/historic-park-museum
The museum was created to preserve and display the rich history of the region and the growth of Frisco from a trapper camp to a thriving mountain community. Displays include a schoolhouse museum, women's fashions from the early 1900s, and a diorama of the train and town. FREE

Groceries/Supplies

Safeway[N] - 1008 Summit Blvd. (970) 668-5144

More Info

Summit County Public Library – Main[O]
37 Peak 1 Drive. (970) 668-5555
www.co.summit.co.us/library

Hospital/Emergency Care: St. Anthony's Summit Medical Center - 340 Peak 1 Drive. (970) 668-3300
www.summitmedicalcenter.org

Info Center[P] - 300 Main Street. (970) 668-5547 OR 800-424-1554   www.townoffrisco.com

Other Fun Stuff

Frisco Bay Marina[Q] -
902 E. Main Street. (970) 668-4334
www.townoffrisco.com/frisco-bay-marina
The Frisco Bay Marina is a full-service marina on the shores of Dillon Reservoir, offering boat rentals of all sorts, tours, sailboat lessons, the Lake Dillon Water Taxi and more.

Directions

From I-70 exit 201 puts you right on Main St, and exit 203 takes you to CO-9

Also, CO-9 from the south turns into Summit Boulevard in town.

Frisco

- A. Marina Park – 900 Main St, on Dillon Reservoir
- B. Walter Byron Memorial Park – 306 Creekside Dr
- C. Meadow Creek Park – 828 Meadow Drive (behind Wal-Mart)
- D. Ten Mile Creek – best access at Walter Byron Memorial Park
- E. Willow Preserve – from Summit Blvd./CO-9, turn east onto Ten Mile Drive
- F. Rainbow Lake – trailhead at 2nd Ave & Belford St
- G. Abbey's Coffee – 720 Main Street
- H. Backcountry Brewery – 720 Main Street
- I. Butterhorn Bakery and Café – 408 Main Street
- J. Deli Belly's – 275 Main Street
- K. The Island Grill – 900 Main Street
- L. Log Cabin Café – 121 Main Street
- M. Frisco Historic Park & Museum – 120 Main Street
- N. Safeway – 1008 Summit Blvd.
- O. Summit County Public Library – Main – 37 Peak One Drive
- P. Info Center – 300 Main Street
- Q. Frisco Marina – 902 E. Main Street

Georgetown
"Silver Queen of the Rockies"

Georgetown has its roots in silver mining. Today, it is a quaint, quiet town that has managed to preserve its old-fashioned charm (and it has the best playground in Colorado!).

The Place to Go

City Park [A] - (Between 9th and 11th on Rose) This park has, hands-down, the best playground in Colorado. Adults and kids alike will love exploring the enormous fort-like structure with its many bridges and stairs and places to climb. There's even a play area for smaller children, with a wooden train and sand box. You'll also find plenty of shade and picnic tables.

Splash Spot

Georgetown Lake - Along the lake there are plenty of places to stop, some even with restrooms.

Trails for Strollers & Little Folks

Square Top Lakes [B] - Aside from a walk downtown, this trail on Guanella Pass is a great place to meaner around (no strollers, though) if everyone's up for the 10-mile drive. Once on the pass, however, the views are stunning because the trailhead sits at 11,669 feet. Chances are little legs won't make it to the lakes (2+ miles), but the walk through the alpine tundra is a fantastic journey.

Kid-Friendly Eateries
(with something for adults too!)

Ed's 1859 Café [C] - 410 6th Street. (303) 569-5042
Nothin' fancy, but everything's good. Ed's serves burgers, burritos and breakfast, plus coffee.

End of the Line [D] - 503 6th St. (303) 569-2058
Stop in at the soda fountain for malts and milkshakes!

Georgetown Valley Candy Company [E] - 500 6th Street. (303) 569-2778
www.shopgvcc.com   Yum...hand-made candies, and lots of chocolate.

Mountain Buzz Cafe [F] - 1200 Argentine Street (303) 569-2020   Breakfast burritos, bagels, vegetarian dishes, paninis, smoothies and all kinds of coffee drinks.

Things to do in Bad Weather

Hamill House Museum [G] - 305 Argentine St. (303)569-2840   www.historicgeorgetown.org
The house was originally constructed in the late 1800s according to the specifications of the town's most famous silver baron, William A. Hamill, using the finest materials available at the time. The Gothic Revival-style building is now open to visitors to display 19th century living, including walnut woodwork, hand-painted wallpaper and imported marble fireplaces. $

Energy Museum [H] - 600 Griffith Street. (303)569-3557 www.georgetownenergymuseum.org
The museum is inside an operating hydroelectric plant built in 1900. Guests can see numerous exhibits (such as 100-year old equipment and consumer appliances) and photographs relating to the early use of electricity, as well as learn about the early development of electricity in Colorado. FREE

Groceries/Supplies

Georgetown Market [I] - 1202 Argentine Street (303) 569-2464

Kneisel & Anderson Grocery [J] - 511 6th Street. (303) 569-2650

More Info

John Tomay Memorial Library [K] - 605 6th Street. (303) 569-2620

Hospital/Emergency Care: *Meadows Family Medical Center* - 115 15th Avenue, Idaho Springs. (303) 567-2668

St. Anthony's Summit Medical Center - 340 Peak 1 Drive, Frisco. (970) 668-3300
www.summitmedicalcenter.org

Georgetown Gateway Visitor Center [L] - 1491 Argentine Street. (303) 569-2405
www.georgetown-colorado.org

Other Fun Stuff

Downtown [M] - The downtown area of Georgetown (6th Street) is a National Historic Landmark District. Not only will you find some of the town's well-preserved Victorian charm, but also several great places to eat, and even stops for sweet treats.

Georgetown Loop Railroad [N] -
(888) 456-6777   www.georgetownlooprr.com
Take a ride on the train! A favorite among kids today, the historic stretch of narrow gauge railroad originally operated for passengers and freight between 1899 and 1938. The Colorado Historical Society began restoring the railroad in 1973 and completed it in 1984.

Guanella Pass [O] -
Follow the Guanella Pass Scenic and Historic Byway up the mountain to the alpine zone. The road follows an old wagon route that linked Georgetown and Grant.

Georgetown

Directions

Unless you're coming down off Guanella Pass, there's only one way into town: exit #228 off I-70.

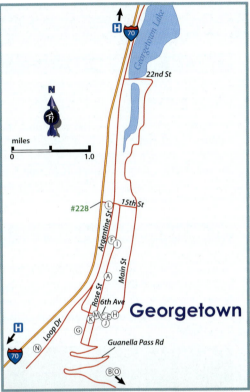

A. City Park – between 9th & 11th on Rose Street
B. Square Top Lakes Trailhead – Guanella Pass, west side of the road
C. Ed's 1859 Café – 410 6th Street
D. End of the Line – 503 6th Street
E. Georgetown Valley Candy Company – 500 6th St
F. Mountain Buzz Café – 1200 Argentine Street
G. Hamill House Museum – 305 Argentine Street
H. Energy Museum – 600 Griffith Street
I. Georgetown Market – 1202 Argentine Street
J. Kneisel & Anderson Grocery – 511 6th Street
K. John Tomay Memorial Library – 605 6th Street
L. Georgetown Gateway Visitor Center - 1491 Argentine Street.
M. Downtown – along 6th St between Argentine and Griffith Streets
N. Georgetown Loop Railroad – Loop Drive to Devil's Gate Station
O. Guanella Pass – 10 miles south of Georgetown on County Rd. 381

Glenwood Springs

"Soak it all in"

Right at the confluence of the Colorado River and the Roaring Fork River, Glenwood Springs is a mecca for outdoor enthusiasts and those seeking to relax in the natural hot springs.

The Place to Go

Veltus Park[A] - (901 Midland Ave) While this isn't the biggest park in town, it is a quiet surprise with a little of everything. Sitting on the **Roaring Fork River**, Veltus Park has a playground, picnic shelters, shade, river access and restrooms.

Other Parks

Two Rivers Park[B] - (740 Devereux Rd) This is the largest park in Glenwood Springs, at the confluence of the **Colorado and Roaring Fork Rivers**. You'll find a great playground, picnic areas, restrooms, access to bike paths, and, of course, places to play in the water.

Axtell Park[C] - (11th and Grand Ave) If you're stopping for visitor information, this is a good bet for a quick run-around, or a picnic. You'll find a playground, shade, picnic tables and restrooms (and yes, visitor information).

Sayre Park (aka Strawberry Park)[D] - (1702 Grand Ave) Sayre Park is quickly accessible from Grand Avenue (CO-82), and offers a playground, shade, covered picnic tables and restrooms.

Glenwood Springs Parks:
www.glenwoodrec.com/city-parks_directory.html

Splash Spots

Colorado River - If you want to play in the CO, your best bet is at **Two Rivers Park**[B].

Roaring Fork River - The river runs the length of town, north to south, offering endless places to cool off. An easy spot to park is at **Veltus Park**[A]. Another option is to walk the **Glenwood Springs River Trail** and let the kids "hunt" for a good spot.

Trails for Strollers & Little Folks

Glenwood Springs River Trail - This paved trail parallels the Roaring Fork River until it connects to the Rio Grande Trail at 23rd Street. Access at **Two Rivers Park**[B] or behind the **Safeway**[M] on the other side of the train tracks.

Glenwood Canyon Trail - Access this trail either from town (start at **Two Rivers Park**[B] and follow 6th St east) or up the road off I-25 (at the Grizzly Creek exit). The path follows the Colorado River for 16 miles, with minimal elevation gain. Once outside of town, you'll see towering canyon walls, raging rapids, limestone and granite cliffs, and maybe even some resident bighorn sheep. Along the way there are four rest areas with restrooms and picnic tables.

Glenwood Springs

Kid-Friendly Eateries
(with something for adults too!)

Glenwood Canyon Brewing Company [E] - 402 7th Street. (970) 945-1276 www.glenwoodcanyon.com
The brewpub is located in the historic Hotel Denver, and serves a variety of food with their hand-crafted beer.

Italian Underground [F] - 715 Grand Avenue. (970) 945-6422 Not a big place, but a delicious one. Good Italian food at affordable prices.

Kaleido Scoops [G] - 1105 Grand Avenue. (970) 945-7338 www.kalscoops.com
They boast the best smoothies in town, and also serve ice cream cones, banana splits, sundaes and the like.

Sacred Grounds [H] - 725 Grand Avenue. (970) 928-8804 www.sacredgrounds.biz
This coffee house and delicatessen serves up great coffee and good eats.

Uncle Pizza [I] - 1826 Grand Avenue. (970) 945-6363 www.unclepizza.com
A local favorite, Uncle's has wonderful pizza, plus salads and sandwiches.

Things to do in Bad Weather

Glenwood Springs Community Center [J] - 100 Wulfsohn Road. (970) 384-6300 www.glenwoodrec.com/community-center.html
This state-of-the-art facility has something for everyone: a rock climbing wall, fitness center, an indoor track, and an aquatics center. The activity pool has zero-depth entry, interactive water features, and a wacky water slide. $

Glenwood Railroad Museum [K] - 413 7th Street (East wing of Train Depot). (970) 945-7044 www.glenwoodrailroadmuseum.org
Trains, trains, trains...everyone LOVES trains! Stop in at the depot to see a large scale model of the Rio Grande steam and diesel trains, a gallery of regional railroad photographs, railroad signals removed from Glenwood Canyon, a Rio Grande rail motorcar, and other such memorabilia and artifacts. $1.00/adults, children FREE.

Glenwood Hot Springs [L] - 415 6th Street. (970) 947-2955 www.hotspringspool.com
The first known people to enjoy the healing powers of the mineral-rich hot springs in Glenwood Springs were the Ute Indians. Ever since, folks have traveled to the area to take advantage of the relaxing waters. Today, the pool spans two city blocks, and is kept between 90-93°. There is also a therapeutic pool that averages 104°, a kiddie pool, a diving pool and a water slide. $

Groceries/Supplies

Safeway [M] - 2001 Grand Avenue. (970) 945-2002

Good Health Downtown Market & Deli [N] 722 Cooper Avenue. (970) 945-0235

City Market [O] - 1410 Grand Ave. (970) 945-8207

More Info

Glenwood Springs Branch Library [P] - 413 9th Street. (970) 945-5958 www.garfieldlibraries.org

Hospital/Emergency Care: Valley View Hospital - 1906 Blake Avenue. (970) 945-6535 www.vvh.org

Visitor's Center: *Glenwood Springs Chamber Resort Association* [Q] - 1102 Grand Avenue. (970) 945-6589 www.visitglenwood.com

Other Fun Stuff

Glenwood Caverns Adventure Park [R] - 51000 Two Rivers Plaza Road. (800) 530-1635 or (970) 945-4228 www.glenwoodcaverns.com
If you have the time and inclination to go to adventure parks, this one offers a lot. At the top of Iron Mountain you'll find thrill rides, laser tag, cave tours, a Wild West Wagon and loads more. Access the park via the Iron Mountain Tram. $

Iron Mountain Tram (part of Glenwood Caverns Adventure Park) [S] - 51000 Two Rivers Plaza Road. (800) 530-1635 or (970) 945-4228 www.glenwoodcaverns.com
Just have a little time? Take a tram ride! The European pulse gondola takes you to the top of Iron Mountain, where you can enjoy spectacular panoramic mountain views, have a picnic, or eat at the mountaintop restaurant. $

Glenwood Springs

Cave Tours (part of Glenwood Caverns Adventure Park)[T] - 51000 Two Rivers Plaza Rd.
(800) 530-1635 or (970) 945-4228
www.glenwoodcaverns.com/glenwood-springs-cave-tours.html

This walking tour of Glenwood Caverns and Historic Fairy Caves was ranked in the top 10 by *USA Today*. The cave formations date back 5 million years, and the tours take you deep into the mountain to explore the giant, wide-open caverns. $

Directions

From the west on I-70, take exit 114. From the east, take exit 116.

From the south, CO-82 turns into Grand Avenue in town.

- A. Veltus Park – 901 Midland Avenue
- B. Two Rivers Park – 740 Devereux Road
- C. Axtell Park – 11th & Grand Avenue (at the Glenwood Springs Chamber Resort)
- D. Sayre Park – 1702 Grand Avenue (best access 1 block east, at N. Hyland Park Drive & Blake Ave)
- E. Glenwood Canyon Brewing Company – 402 7th St
- F. Italian Underground – 715 Grand Avenue
- G. Kaleido Scoops – 1105 Grand Avenue
- H. Sacred Grounds – 725 Grand Avenue
- I. Uncle Pizza – 1826 Grand Avenue
- J. Community Center – 100 Wulfsohn Rd
- K. Glenwood Railroad Museum – 413 7th Street
- L. Glenwood Hot Springs – 415 6th Street
- M. Safeway – 2001 Grand Avenue
- N. Good Health Market & Deli – 722 Cooper Ave
- O. City Market – 1410 Grand Avenue
- P. Glenwood Springs Branch Library – 413 9th St
- Q. Glenwood Springs Chamber Resort Association – 1102 Grand Avenue
- R. Glenwood Caverns Adventure Park – 51000 Two Rivers Plaza Road
- S. Iron Mountain Tram – 51000 Two Rivers Plaza Rd
- T. Cave Tours – 51000 Two Rivers Plaza Road

Golden
"Where the west lives"

Golden was founded during the gold rush in 1859 and even served as the territorial capital for a time in the 1860s. Two large mesas, North and South Table Mountains, separate Golden from the sprawling metropolis of Denver, allowing it to retain its small town identity.

The Place to Go

Lions Park[A] - (1300 10th St) A great park! Not only is the playground newly renovated, but there's plenty of shade, picnic tables, and a duck pond. If that's not enough, the *Clear Creek Trail*, and *Clear Creek* itself, are just across the street. Restrooms available near 10th and Maple.

Another Park

Clear Creek History Park[B] - (11th and Arapahoe) (303) 278-3557 (Golden History Museums) www.goldenhistorymuseums.org/clearcreekpark.php
A visit to this park is like strolling through a frontier ranch. Many of the buildings were relocated from the 1878 Pearce Homestead. You can explore cabins, a schoolhouse, a working blacksmith shop, a root cellar, gardens and a chicken coop (complete with real, 21st century chickens!). FREE

Parfet Park[C] - (725 10th St) Just need a place to lay in the grass or have a picnic? Parfet Park is located right across from the *Visitors Center*[L] and offers lots of grass, shade and public restrooms. There's also easy access to the water and the *Clear Creek Trail* from this park.

Splash Spot

Clear Creek - From *Lions Park*,[A] take a walk up or down the *Clear Creek Trail*. There are many, many, many great places to play in the water. Keep an eye out for boaters playing, too.

Trails for Strollers & Little Folks

Clear Creek Trail - This paved trail follows, yes, Clear Creek. Access at *Lions Park* [A], the *library* [K], the *Visitors Center* [L] or Vanover Park (Water Street & Ford Street).

Kid-Friendly Eateries
(with something for adults too!)

The Alley [D] - 1205 Washington Avenue. (303) 278-6366
The no frills sandwiches are a good solid meal at good prices.

D' Deli at D' Creek [E] - 923 10th Street (creek side, at the Pioneer Museum). (303) 279-8020
www.ddelisubs.coM
Deli sandwiches and a GREAT creek-side deck.

Grappa Mediterranean Bistro [F] - 1027 Washington Avenue. (303) 273-8882
www.grappabistro.com
Serving Mediterranean cuisine for lunch and dinner.

Table Mountain Grill & Cantina [G] - 1310 Washington Avenue. (303) 216-8040
www.tablemountaininn.com/restaurant
Award-winning southwestern food for breakfast, lunch and dinner.

Things to do in Bad Weather

Golden Community Center [H] -
1470 10th Street. (303) 384-8100
The center includes an indoor playground, a leisure pool with a water slide and interactive play areas, a fitness area, and more. $

Colorado Railroad Museum [I] - 17155 W. 44th Avenue. (303) 279-4591 OR 800-365-6263
http://www.coloradorailroadmuseum.org/
A museum and 15 acres of grounds filled with railroad exhibits...the perfect detour. On the grounds there are locomotives and cars to explore, as well as equipment and rails. The museum itself is a replica of an 1880-style depot and contains artifacts, records, artwork and photos depicting the railroads in the Rocky Mountain area. $

Groceries/Supplies

Safeway [J] -
1701 Jackson Street. (303) 278-1861

More Info

Library: Golden Library [K] - 1019 10th Street. (303) 235-5275   http://jefferson.lib.co.us

Hospital/Emergency Care:
St. Anthony Hospital - 11600 W. 2nd Place, Lakewood. (303) 629-4314
www.stanthonyhosp.org

Exempla Lutheran Medical Center - 8300 W. 38th Street, Wheat Ridge. (303) 425-4500
www.exempla.org

Golden Chamber of Commerce & Visitors Center [L] - 1010 Washington Avenue. (303) 279-3113   www.goldenvisitorscenter.net
More Info: www.2hourvacation.com

Other Fun Stuff

Lookout Mountain Nature Center and Preserve [M] - 910 Colorow Road. (720) 497-7600
The Lookout Mountain Nature Center and Preserve offers both indoor and outdoor exploration. Inside, visitors will find exhibits about migrating birds and the ponderosa pine forest. Outside, you can stroll through the forest and meadow on winding trails, have a picnic, or go on a guided nature program. FREE

Splash Aquatic Park [N] - 3151 Illinois Street. 303-277-8700   www.splashingolden.com
This isn't a quick stop, but it sure is a whole lotta fun! Zoom down a twisty-turny water slide, play in the activity pool fountains, climb on the jungle-gym, dig in the sand on the "beach," cool off in the spray fountain, or simply relax under an awning. $

Golden

Directions

From the north, take CO-93 south to Washington Avenue (the mainstreet through town). This will take you to downtown.

From the east, take CO-58 west to Washington Ave, then head south.

From the south, take US-6 north to 19th Street. Follow 19th east to Washington Avenue and turn left.

From the west, US-6 east turns into CO-58. Exit at Washington Avenue and head south.

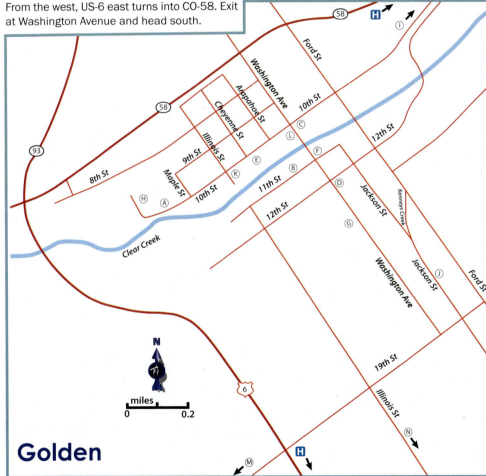

A. Lions Park – 1300 10th Street
B. Clear Creek History Park – 11th & Arapahoe
C. Parfet Park – 725 10th Street
D. The Alley – 1205 Washington Avenue
E. D' Deli at D' Creek – 923 10th Street
F. Grappa Mediterranean Bistro – 1027 Washington Avenue
G. Table Mountain Grill & Cantina – 1310 Washington Avenue
H. Golden Community Center – 1470 10th Street
I. Colorado Railroad Museum – 17155 W. 44th Ave
J. Safeway – 1701 Jackson Street
K. Golden Library – 1019 10th Street
L. Golden Visitors Center – 1010 Washington Ave
M. Lookout Mountain Nature Center and Preserve – 910 Colorow Rd.
N. Splash Aquatic Park – 3151 Illinois Street

Granby

"The Heart of Something Grand"

Granby, which prides itself on its friendly, small-town atmosphere, sits in a large valley surrounded by national forest, with views of Rocky Mountain National Park and the Continental Divide.

The Place to Go

Granby Elementary School A - (202 W. Topaz Ave) If school is not in session, a stop at this playground is mandatory...it's easily one of the best in Colorado. Really. From Agate Avenue (the main road through town), the turrets on the playground are easily visible. The kids will be able to entertain themselves for hours on the endless wooden structures that are full of bridges, slides, ropes, hiding places, and climbing challenges. There's also a covered picnic table. Public restrooms are available across the street at the park.

Another Park

Kaibab Park B - (on CR-574, south of town) As you turn off US-40 following the signs, you'll feel like you missed something. However, on the left is a bridge leading to the park where you'll find a playground, restrooms, a picnic shelter, a kids' fishing pond and water access.

Granby

Splash Spots

Fraser River ^C - The river is easily accessible from either the east or west side of US-40, on the south end of town, south of the bridge. Best bet is at *Kaibab Park* ^B.

Rainbow Bay Picnic Site ^D - On the southwest edge of Lake Granby, north of town, this picnic site is a great little get-away with access to the lake shore. Take US-34 north 6 miles to CR 6/Arapahoe Bay Rd; parking is one mile up on the left.

Trails for Strollers & Little Folks

Fraser to Granby Trail ^E - Thanks to the efforts of the Headwaters Trails Alliance, this trail connects Granby, Fraser and Winter Park. In Granby, access the trail south of town at *Kaibab Park* ^B.

Kid-Friendly Eateries
(with something for adults too!)

Brickhouse 40 ^F - 320 E. Agate Avenue.
(970) 887-3505
Voted the best of Grand County, Brickhouse 40 serves steaks, pasta, and Italian and Greek specials.

Ian's Mountain Bakery ^G - 358 E. Agate Ave.
(970) 887-1176
Stop in for amazing pastries, baked goods, breakfast burritos, sandwiches, coffee and more. And even gluten-free pizza!

Java Lava ^H - 200 W. Agate Avenue.
(970) 887-9810
Not just java…breakfast all day long, too!

Maverick's Grille ^I - 15 E. Agate Avenue.
(970) 887-9000   www.mavericksgrille.com
Specializing in family dining, they serve a tasty selection of steaks, chicken, burgers and game.

Things to do in Bad Weather

Grand Park Community Recreation Center ^J - 1 Main Street, Fraser.
(970) 726-8968   www.fraservalleyrec.org
It's not in town, but worth the 15 mile drive to Fraser. The family leisure pool in the rec center has a 20-foot water slide, spraying water features, a lazy river, and zero-depth entry. The center also includes a gymnasium, weight room, indoor track and more. $

Groceries/Supplies

City Market ^K - 1001 Thompson Dr.
(970) 887-7140

More Info

Library: Granby Library ^L - 55 Zero Street.
(970) 887-2149

Hospital/Emergency Care:
Granby Medical Center - 480 E. Agate Ave.
(970) 887-2117   www.stanthonymountainclinics.org

The Greater Granby Area Chamber of Commerce ^M - 365 E. Agate Ave. (970) 887-2311 OR (800) 325-1661   www.granbychamber.com

Other Fun Stuff

Beacon Landing Marina ^N - 1026 CR 64.
(970) 627-3671 OR (800) 864-4372
http://beaconlanding.us
This marina is on the north shore of Lake Granby, 12 miles north of town. Follow US-34 north to CR-64. The marina offers boat rentals for fishing, sight-seeing or wildlife viewing on Lake Granby.

Hot Sulphur Springs Resort & Spa ^O - 5609 CR 20, Hot Sulphur Springs. (970) 725-3306 OR (800) 510-6235   www.hotsulphursprings.com
If there isn't an immediate need to exit the car, take the drive to Hot Sulphur Springs (10 miles west on US-40) to visit one of the nation's oldest and largest natural hot mineral springs. There are 21 mineral pools and baths, at temperatures between 95-112°, although children are limited to 4 pools. $

Granby

Directions

Granby is on US-40, north of Fraser and Winter Park.

US-34 intersects US-40 just west of town.

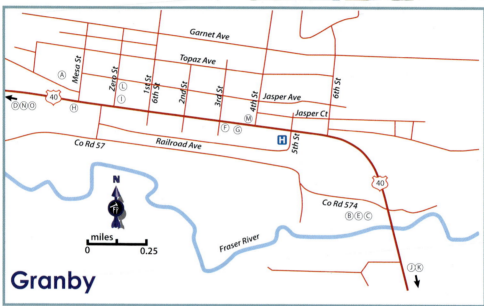

A. Granby Elementary School – 202 W. Topaz Ave
B. Kaibab Park – CR 574, off US-40 on the south end of town, south of the bridge
C. Fraser River – Access at Kaibab Park
D. Rainbow Bay Picnic Site – 6 miles north of Granby, on Arapahoe Bay Rd.
E. Fraser to Granby Trail – Kaibab Park
F. Brickhouse 40 – 320 E. Agate
G. Ian's Mountain Bakery – 358 E. Agate
H. Java Lava – 200 W. Agate
I. Maverick's Grille – 15 E. Agate Avenue
J. Grand Park Community Recreation Center – 1 Main Street, Fraser
K. City Market – 1001 Thompson Dr. (along US-40)
L. Granby Library – 55 Zero Street
M. The Great Granby Area Chamber of Commerce – 365 East Agate Avenue
N. Beacon Landing – 1026 CR 64, Grand Lake
O. Hot Sulphur Springs Resort & Spa – 5609 CR 20, Hot Sulphur Springs

Grand Junction
"Colorado's Wine Country"

Grand Junction sits on Colorado's Western Slope, just as the mountains give way to the Utah desert.

The Place to Go

Canyon View Park A - (730 24 Rd) For those traveling the interstate, this 110-acre park at exit 28 is PERFECT. It couldn't be easier to access, and has all the amenities: large playground, covered picnic tables, paths for a walk, public restrooms, and even a duck pond!

Other Parks

Duck Pond Park B - (415 Santa Clara) If you are coming to Grand Junction from the south, this park is a convenient stopping spot off US-50 before you get into town. You'll find a playground, grassy areas, picnic tables, public restrooms and walking paths.

Emerson Park C - (9th and Ute Ave) Not far from downtown, this park has a playground, picnic tables, shade, grassy areas and public restrooms.

Hawthorne Park D - (4th and Gunnison) Another great option for rest and play among old shade trees. Hawthorne Park has a large playground, picnic tables and public restrooms.

Lincoln Park E - (12th and Gunnison) While this 42-acre park is a bit removed from downtown, it has a public outdoor pool and lots of open space to play. You'll also find a playground, picnic shelter, restrooms and a track.

Riverside Park F - (675 W. Colorado Ave) Riverside Park is yes, on the river and the **Colorado River Trail**. There is also a playground, a shelter, and restrooms.

Grand Junction Parks:
www.gjcity.org/Parks_Maintenance.aspx

Splash Spots

Colorado River - Jump on the *Colorado River Trail* to find spots for rock-throwing or wading.

Lincoln Park-Moyer Pool G - (1340 Gunnison Ave) www.gjcity.org/CityDeptWebPages/Parks Recreation/Aquatics/LPPool.htm
This outdoor pool has a 37-foot tall water slide, a splash pad water playground and diving boards. $

Trails for Strollers & Little Folks

Colorado River Trail - The paved Colorado River Trail follows the river through town. Easy access points include at the *Western Colorado Botanical Gardens* H and *Riverside Park* F.

Connected Lakes (Colorado River State Park) I - Take Broadway/Hwy-340 to Power Road, travel northwest; continue on Dike Road to the park. This is one of several sections of the Colorado River State Park, and the one closest to Grand Junction. It offers LOADS of trails, both paved and unpaved, as well as picnic tables, restrooms, fishing and water access. $

Trail Through Time (at Rabbit Valley) J - If you're heading past Exit 2 on I-70, stop here. The interpretive trail here is 1.5 miles long, and offers a glimpse of a time when dinosaurs lived in Colorado. You'll see fossils and bones, including that of a diplodocus and camarasaurus, and pass a working fossil quarry.

Kid-Friendly Eateries
(with something for adults too!)

Enstrom Candies K - 701 Colorado Avenue. (970) 683-1000   www.enstrom.com
A locally owned business that's been handed down through generations. Famous for its almond toffee and other candies.

Gelato Junction L - 449 Main Street (downtown). (970) 245-4759   www.gelatojunction.com
Great place for a cold sweet treat if you're wandering around downtown.

Main Street Café M - 504 Main Street (downtown). (970) 242-7225   www.mainstreetcafegj.com
Serving the finest and freshest foods available, this classic diner also offers a unique atmosphere.

Pablo's Pizza N - 319 Main Street (downtown). (970) 255-8879   www.pablospizza.com
This pizzeria was inspired by Picasso...really. Their pizzas are "revolutionary creations," and they even have gluten-free crusts available.

Rockslide Brewery O - 401 Main Street (downtown). (970) 245-2111   www.rockslidebrewpub.com
Great place for burgers and brews, and a designated gluten-free menu too!

Starbucks (drive thru!) P - 624 Rae Lynn (at F Rd & 24 Rd). (970) 241-1093
This is strategically located right down the road from *Canyon View Park* A, just off I-70 at exit 28.

Things to do in Bad Weather

KidzPlex Fun & Fitness Center Q - 609 25 Rd. (970)245-3610   www.kidzplex.com
KidzPlex is a multi-purpose children's place, including a soft indoor playground with a zip line, mountain climbs, mazes, and more. $ (although parents are free).

The Museum of Western Colorado R - 462 Ute Avenue (downtown).   (970) 242-0971 www.museumofwesternco.com/visit/museum-of-the-west
Travel back in time to discover the real Wild West. Exhibits include a stagecoach, Anasazi artifacts, firearms used by outlaws, a 1921 LaFrance fire truck, and interactive stations. $

Grand Junction

Orchard Mesa Community Center Pool ^{S} - 2736 Unaweep Avenue. (970) 254-3885
The unique Z-shaped indoor pool here has a 2-foot wading area, waterslide, diving boards and a hot tub. $

Groceries/Supplies

Vitamin Cottage ^{T} - 2464 US-50 & US-6. (970) 263-7750

Safeway ^{U} - 681 Horizon Drive (exit 31 off I-70). (970) 254-0227

City Market ^{V} - 200 Rood Ave. (970) 241-2278

More Info

Library: Central Library ^{W} - 530 Grand Avenue. (970) 243-4783 www.mcpld.org

Hospital/Emergency Care: St. Mary's Hospital & Regional Medical Center - 2635 North 7th Street. (970) 298-2273 www.stmarygj.com

Grand Junction Visitor and Convention Bureau ^{X} - 740 Horizon Drive. (800) 962-2547 http://www.visitgrandjunction.com/

Other Fun Stuff

Bananas Fun Park ^{Y} - 2469 Riverside Parkway (970) 241-7529 www.bananasfunpark.com
Let your monkeys run wild at this indoor-outdoor family entertainment center. Activities include bumper boats, batting cages, Go-Karts, an inflatable playground, laser tag and other fun stuff. $

Colorado National Monument ^{Z} - Monument Road, Fruita. (970) 858-3617 www.nps.gov/colm
Just a few miles from Grand Junction, Colorado National Monument is a fascinating landscape of deep canyons, towering monoliths, vast plateaus, and red-rock cliffs, and home to many types of wildlife.

Dinosaur Digs ^{AA} - 550 Jurasic Court, Fruita. (888) 488-DINO www.museumofwesternco.com/dino-digs
Take the kids to dig for dinosaurs! A real paleontologist leads the expedition in a dinosaur quarry to search for fossils, bones and tracks. Only for children 5 and older. $

Dinosaur Journey Museum ^{BB} - 550 Jurassic Court, Fruita (exit 19). (970) 858-7282 www.museumofwesternco.com/visit/dinosaur-journey/
Dinosaurs fans will love this hands-on, interactive museum that includes robotic displays, real dinosaur bones that were found in Colorado and a full-size skeleton. $

Directions

I-70 will get you there from the east or west.

From the south, follow US-50 into town; it turns into 5th Street.

Grand Junction

A. Canyon View Park – 730 24 Road
B. Duck Pond Park – 415 Santa Clara
C. Emerson Park – 9th Street & Ute Avenue
D. Hawthorne Park – 4th & Gunnison
E. Lincoln Park – 12th Street & Gunnison Avenue
F. Riverside Park – 675 W. Colorado Avenue
G. Lincoln Park-Moyer Pool – 1340 Gunnison Ave
H. Western Colorado Botanical Gardens – 641 Struthers Avenue (southern end of 7th St)
I. Connected Lakes - Take Broadway/Hwy 340 to Power Road, travel northwest; continue on Dike Road to the park
J. Trail Through Time – Exit 2 on I-70
K. Enstrom Candies – 701 Colorado Avenue
L. Gelato Junction – 449 Main Street
M. Main Street Café – 504 Main Street
N. Pablo's Pizza – 319 Main Street
O. Rockslide Brewery – 401 Main Street
P. Starbucks Drive Thru – 624 Rae Lynn
Q. KidzPlex – 609 25 Rd.
R. The Museum of Western Colorado – 462 Ute Ave
S. Orchard Mesa Community Center Pool – 2736 Unaweep Avenue
T. Vitamin Cottage – 2464 US-50/US-6/I-70 Business Loop
U. Safeway – 681 Horizon Drive
V. City Market – 200 Rood Avenue
W. Mesa County Public Library – 530 Grand Avenue
X. Grand Junction Visitor and Convention Bureau – 740 Horizon Drive
Y. Bananas Fun Park – 2469 Riverside Parkway
Z. Colorado National Monument – Monument Road, Fruita
AA. Dinosaur Digs – 550 Jurassic Court, Fruita
BB. Dinosaur Journey Museum – 550 Jurassic Court, Fruita

Grand Lake

The historic village of Grand Lake sits on the north shore of Grand Lake and in the shadow of the Continental Divide one mile from the western entrance to Rocky Mountain National Park. This small town offers big adventures on both water and mountains, as well as a true taste of the west.

The Place to Go

Lakeside Park [A] - (Along Lake Ave.) A sandy beach in Colorado! The water may be a bit cold, but the kids never seem to care. Bring buckets and shovels for sand castles. There are also picnic tables, two marinas to rent boats from, and public restrooms.

The Place to Go, Take Two

Grand Lake Boardwalk [B] - If you are looking for "one stop stopping," park downtown. Along the historic boardwalk you'll find many spots for food, drinks or treats, and to absorb the spirit of the Wild West. Along Grand Avenue you'll also find *Town Square Park* [C] which is the site of many festivals and events in the summer. There's a playground, the Heckert Pavilion, public restrooms, the community house and *Juniper Library* [O].

Trails for Strollers & Little Folks

Adams Falls [E] - On the east side of Grand Lake, less than a mile from the middle of the village, a short walk brings you to Adams Falls, a beautiful waterfall that feeds into Grand Lake.

East Shore [F] - A lovely, relatively unknown trail that follows the shore line of Shadow Mountain Reservoir.

Kid-Friendly Eateries
(with something for adults too!)

Bear's Den [G] - *612 Grand Ave. (970) 627-3385* They serve up Grandma's old fashioned breakfast, lunch and dinner, including a "little bears" menu.

Blue Water Bakery [H] - *928 Grand Avenue (970) 627-5416* A quick stop for coffee or treats.

Splash Spot

Point Park National Recreation Area [D] - If you want to splash away from the crowds downtown at *Lakeside Park* [A], try this lovely lakeside spot, tucked away in a quiet part of town. There are covered picnic tables, and restrooms also.

The Grand Lake Brewing Company ^I -
915 Grand Avenue. (970) 627-1711
www.grandlakebrewing.com

The beer is made from the fresh headwaters of the Colorado River, and the food is good too!

Grand Lake Chocolates ^J - 918 Grand Ave. (970) 627-9494   www.grandlakechocolates.com

The line may be out the door this place is so popular, but they are quick and it's worth the wait.

Miyauchi's Snack Bar ^K - 1029 Lake Avenue. (970) 627-9319

This snack bar is strategically located across the street from *Lakeside Park* ^A for a quick ice cream or snack.

Sagebrush BBQ and Grill ^L - 1101 Grand Avenue. (970) 627-1404   www.sagebrushbbq.com

Finger-lickin' good barbeque in an authentic old west setting.

Things to do in Bad Weather

Kauffman House Museum ^M - At Pitkin Street and Lake Avenue. (970) 627-9644
www.kauffmanhouse.org

The Grand Lake Area Historical Society maintains the museum, which operated as a hotel between 1892 and 1946. It is the only remaining log hotel built in Grand Lake before 1900, and is listed in the National Register of Historic Places. Donations accepted.

Grand Lake Lanes ^N - 824 Grand Avenue.
(970) 627-3373   www.grandlakelanes.com

If the kids are old enough, and the weather's that bad, try a few frames of bowling. They serve pizza, too. $

Groceries/Supplies

Mountain Food Market ^O - 400 Grand Avenue. (970) 627-3470

More Info

Library: *Juniper Library at Grand Lake* ^P - 316 Garfield Street, at Town Square Park. (970) 627-8353
www.gcld.org/content/locations/juniper

Hospital/Emergency Care: *Granby Medical Center* - 480 E. Agate Avenue, Granby. (970) 887-2117 www.stanthonymountainclinics.org

Grand Lake Chamber of Commerce ^Q - Corner of West Portal Rd. & US-34. (970) 627-3372 OR (800)531-1019   www.grandlakechamber.com

Other Fun Stuff

Grand Lake Marina ^R - 1246 Lake Avenue. (970) 627-9273
http://www.glmarina.com/

Boats for rent at this marina include pontoons, fishing boats, kayaks, speed boats and Boston Whalers. Coffee and food are also available there at The Wake. $

Grand Lake 85

Headwaters Marina ˢ - 1030 Lake Avenue.
(970) 627-5031
www.townofgrandlake.com/headwaters-marina.htm
Take a historic lake tour from this marina, or rent your own (many types to choose from) including pontoons, fishing, pedal and bumper boats. They also have a small arcade. $

Rocky Mountain Repertory Theatre ᵀ -
404 Vine Street. (970) 627-3421
www.rockymountainrep.com
This theatre has become an integral part of the arts and culture of Grand Lake. Performances of all varieties available, including shows performed by the youth theatre. $

Sombrero Stables ᵁ - 304 West Portal Road.
(970) 627-3514   www.sombrero.com
A visit to the Wild West might need to include a horseback ride! Children under 5 can ride double in a saddle with an adult. $

Rocky Mountain National Park ⱽ -
(970) 627-3471
On the west side of the park, the Kawuneeche Visitor Center on US-34 is a mile north of Grand Lake. There are many wonderful hikes on this side of the park (try the Colorado River Trailhead to Lulu City...little legs will love it), and also loads of opportunities to spot moose. $

Directions

Grand Lake is located just off US-34, near the west entrance to Rocky Mountain National Park.

Grand Lake

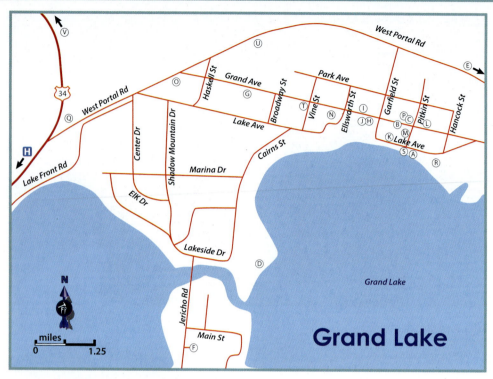

A. Lakeside Park – on the shore of Grand Lake, along Lake Avenue between Hancock and Ellsworth Streets
B. Grand Lake Boardwalk – along Grand Avenue in town, from Ellsworth Street to Hancock Street
C. Town Square Park - at the center of town on Grand Avenue
D. Point Park National Recreation Area – west side of Grand Lake, Cairns Avenue to Shadow Mountain Lane
E. Adams Falls trailhead – Follow W. Portal Rd. east to E. Inlet Trailhead parking
F. East Shore Trailhead – Jericho Road (take Jeicho 0.5mi to the stop sign at Shore Landing; turn left.)
G. Bear's Den – 612 Grand Avenue
H. Blue Water Bakery -928 Grand Avenue
I. The Grand Lake Brewing Company – 915 Grand Avenue
J. Grand Lake Chocolates – 918 Grand Avenue
K. Miyauchi's Snack Bar – 1029 Lake Avenue
L. Sagebrush BBQ and Grill – 1101 Grand Avenue
M. Kauffman House Museum – Pitkin Street & Lake Avenue
N. Grand Lake Lanes – 824 Grand Avenue
O. Mountain Food Market – 400 Grand Avenue
P. Juniper Library at Grand Lake – 316 Garfield Street, on Town Square Park
Q. Grand Lake Chamber of Commerce – 14700 US-34
R. Grand Lake Marina – 1246 Lake Avenue
S. Headwaters Marina – 1030 Lake Avenue
T. Rocky Mountain Repertory Theatre – 404 Vine St
U. Sombrero Stables – 304 West Portal Road
V. Rocky Mountain National Park – Kawuneeche Visitor Center, US-34 1 mile north of Grand Lake

Gunnison

The west is alive and well in this active ranching community in the Gunnison Valley. The town is also known for its outstanding outdoor recreational opportunities along the Gunnison River, in the West Elk Range or on some of the hundreds of thousands of acres of public lands surrounding the city.

The Place to Go

Legion Park A - (500 E Tomichi Ave) Legion Park is right on US-50/Tomichi Avenue, making a stop here super easy. There's lots of space to run around, several play structures (including a new one with multiple levels), restrooms and picnic tables underneath old shade trees. The visitor center is also in the southwest corner of the park.

Trails for Strollers & Little Folks

Hartman Rocks C - This recreation area is a mix of dirt roads and single track trails, ranging from easy to moderate. The length of your hike is up to you. The trails take you through rolling hills of sagebrush, cottonwood groves and granite rock formations.

Splash Spot

Blue Mesa Reservoir B - Blue Mesa is Colorado's largest body of water and offers many opportunities for splashing, fishing and boating. Good wading/swimming spots include Bay of Chickens (1.2 miles west of Elk Creek), Dry Creek (1 mile east of Elk Creek) and Old Highway 50 Beach (adjacent to the Elk Creek Campground). FREE

Neversink D - This 1 mile hike is ADA accessible, meaning it's a great stroll for small kids either under their own power or stroller power. The trail is along the north shore of the Gunnison River, among grasses, wildflowers and cottonwoods.

Kid-Friendly Eateries
(with something for adults too!)

The Bean Coffeehouse & Eatery E - 120 N. Main Street. (970) 641-2408
www.thebeancoffeehouseandeatery.com
The Bean is a local favorite. They serve great coffee and great food (breakfast burritos, sandwiches, etc.), and also have a kid corner with toys to play with.

The Firebrand Delicatessen F - 108 N. Main Street. (970) 641-6266
Delicious subs to eat in or take out.

Garlic Mike's G - 2674 N. Highway 135. (970) 641-2493   www.garlicmikes.com
Just north of town, Garlic Mikes won the people's choice award for the Best Fine Dining many years running.

The Gunnison Brewery H - 138 N. Main Street. (970) 641-2739   www.gunnisonbrewery.com
A simple bar menu and good beer.

Things to do in Bad Weather

Gunnison Community and Aquatics Center I - 200 E. Spencer Avenue. (970) 641-8060
www.gunnisonrec.com
This new center is a good hideout in bad weather. Try out the leisure pool and water slides, climb the rock wall, or burn some energy in the tumbling room. $

Pioneer Museum J - 803 E. Tomichi Avenue. (970) 641-4530
Kids can climb on a Denver & Rio Grande railroad engine and other train cars, and even ring the train bell. Also on the grounds of the museum are an old post office, a schoolhouse and many more original outbuildings full of historical artifacts. $

Groceries/Supplies

City Market K - 880 N. Main St. (970) 641-3816

Safeway L - 112 S. Spruce. (970) 641-0787

More Info

Library: Gunnison County Public Library M - 307 N. Wisconsin Street. (970) 641-3485

Hospital/Emergency Care: *Gunnison Valley Hospital* - 711 North Taylor Street, Gunnison. (970) 641-1456   www.gvh-colorado.org

Gunnison Country Chamber of Commerce N - 500 E. Tomichi Avenue. (970) 641-1501
www.gunnison-co.com

More Info:
www.gunnisoncrestedbutte.com

Other Fun Stuff

Curecanti National Recreation Area O - (970) 641-2337   www.nps.gov/cure
Blue Mesa Reservoir is at the heart of the recreation area, but there are also many places for hiking, camping, picnicking, boating and wildlife viewing. Stop at the Elk Creek Visitors Center (on US-50, west of CO-149) for more information.

Directions

Gunnison lies at the intersection of US-50 and CO-135.

Gunnison

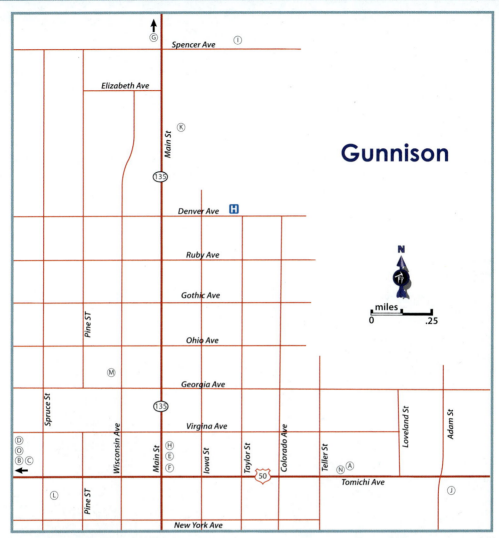

A. Legion Park – 500 E. Tomichi Avenue
B. Blue Mesa Reservoir – west of town on US-50
C. Hartman Rocks - West on US-50, 1/2 mile west of town, before you cross the Gunnison River, turn left onto Gold Basin Road (CR 38). Travel 2.8 miles to the sign marking the entrance to the Hartman Rocks Recreation Area.
D. Neversink - West on Highway 50 for 5 miles. The entrance is on the south side of the highway and is well marked.
E. The Bean Coffeehouse & Eatery – 120 N. Main St
F. The Firebrand Delicatessen – 108 N. Main Street
G. Garlic Mike's – 2674 N. Highway 135
H. The Gunnison Brewery – 138 N. Main Street
I. Gunnison Community and Aquatics Center – 200 E. Spencer Avenue
J. Pioneer Museum – 803 E. Tomichi Avenue
K. City Market – 880 N. Main Street
L. Safeway – 112 S. Spruce Street
M. Gunnison County Public Library – 307 N. Wisconsin Street
N. Visitor's Center/Gunnison Country Chamber of Commerce – 500 E. Tomichi Avenue
O. Curecanti National Recreation Area – west of Gunnison on US-50

Idaho Springs
"Gem of the Mountains"

Idaho Springs, only 30 miles west of Denver, is a portal to mountain adventure. The town was founded in the early days of the Pikes Peak Gold Rush, and today the Downtown Historic District is on the National Register of Historic Places.

The Place to Go

City Hall [A] - (1711 Miner St) Behind city hall kids will enjoy climbing on Engine #60. This stop also includes shade, a path under I-70 to the Charlie Tayler water wheel, and a short walk to downtown and many dining choices.

Park

Courtney-Ryley-Cooper Park [B] - (On Colorado Blvd, just east of 23rd Ave) This brand new playground by the river is completely fenced in, and includes a shaded picnic shelter, large trees, and a Subway right next door. There are public restrooms across the street near the *Visitor Center* [P].

Splash Spot

Clear Creek - Best bet for a quick cool-down in Idaho Springs is near the picnic pavilion at *Courtney-Ryley-Cooper Parks* [B]

Idaho Springs 91

Kid-Friendly Eateries
(with something for adults too!)

Beau Jo's Pizza ^C - *1517 Miner Street. (303)567-4376   www..beaujos.com*
Legendary mountain pies including a gluten-free option.

Georgetown Valley Candy Company ^D
1501 Miner Street. (720) 242-9524
Treats for everyone!

Hilldaddy's Wildfire Restaurant ^E -
2910 Colorado Boulevard. (303) 567-2775
A local favorite with great BBQ.

Java Mountain Roasters Coffee ^F - *1510 Miner Street. (303) 567-0304   www.jmrcoffee.com*
JMR is a family-owned coffeehouse and roastery, offering unique coffees and blends.

Starbucks (drive thru) ^G -
2900 Colorado Boulevard. (303) 567-2578

Tommyknocker Brewery & Pub ^H -
1401 Miner Street. (303)567-2688
www.tommyknocker.com
Home to award-winning, hand-crafted beer and good pub fare.

Two Brothers Deli ^I - *1424 Miner Street. (303) 567-2439   www.twobrothersdeli.com*
Fantastic sandwiches, pizzas, and breakfasts.

Things to do in Bad Weather

Indian Hot Springs Resort ^J -
302 Soda Creek Road. (303) 989-6666
www.indianhotsprings.com
The hot springs-fed pool at this resort is under a translucent dome and surrounded by flowering plants and palm trees, creating a tropical paradise. The temperature is kept at 90+ degrees. $ (but children 5 and under are FREE)

Argo Gold Mine and Mill ^K - *2350 Riverside Dr. (303) 567-2421   www.historicargotours.com*
Take a tour of the historic mine and mill, and learn about the tunnel that connects Idaho Springs to Black Hawk. The tours include a demonstration of crushing, milling and drilling rock. Artifacts used by the miners are on display in the mill. $

Recreation Center ^L - *1130 Idaho Street. (303) 567-4822   www.clearcreekrecreation.com*
Swing from a Tarzan rope, dive off the board, wade with the little ones, and just relax. $

Groceries/Supplies

Safeway ^M - *2425 Miner Street. (303) 567-4471*

92 Idaho Springs

More Info

Idaho Springs Public Library N - 219 14th Avenue. 303-567-2020

Hospital/Emergency Care: Meadows Family Medical Center O - 115 15th Avenue. (303) 567-2668

Exempla Lutheran Medical Center - 8300 W. 38th Avenue, Wheat Ridge. (303) 425-4500   www.exempla.org

Idaho Springs Visitor Center P - 2060 Miner St. (303) 567-4660   www.idahospringsco.com

Other Fun Stuff

Heritage Museum Q - 2060 Miner Street. (303) 567-4382
www.historicidahosprings.com/attractions

The museum displays artifacts dating back to the 1860s and the gold rush that transformed the area. There are also displays of Native American objects, fire-fighting equipment, mining tools, and other items from everyday life of the time period. FREE

Directions

From I-70 use Exit 241 for fast food, 240 for downtown.

Idaho Springs

A. Idaho Springs City Hall – 1711 Miner Street
B. Courtney-Ryley-Cooper Parks – on Colorado Blvd., just east of 23rd Avenue
C. Beau Jo's Pizza – 1517 Miner Street
D. Georgetown Valley Candy Company – 1501 Miner St
E. Hilldaddy's Wildfire Restaurant – 2910 Colorado Blvd.
F. Java Mountain Roasters Coffee – 1510 Miner St
G. Starbucks Drive-Thru – 2900 Colorado Blvd.
H. Tommyknocker Brewery & Pub – 1401 Miner St
I. Two Brothers Deli – 1424 Miner Street
J. Indian Hot Springs Resort – 302 Soda Creek Rd
K. Argo Gold Mine & Mill – 2350 Riverside Drive
L. Recreation Center – 1130 Idaho Street
M. Safeway – 2425 Miner Street
N. Idaho Springs Public Library – 219 14th Avenue
O. Meadows Family Medical Center – 115 15th Ave
P. Idaho Springs Visitors Center – 2060 Miner Street
Q. Heritage Museum – 2060 Miner Street

Kremmling

Kremmling lies at the confluence of three rivers (the Blue River, Muddy Creek and the Colorado River) and is surrounded by thousands of acres of BLM and Forest Service land, making it a great destination for outdoor adventures.

The Place to Go

Veterans Memorial Park [A] - (12th and Park Ave) Stop here for something a little different. Aside from a small playground and picnic shelter, there is a memorial at the southwest corner of the park commemorating Kremmling veterans. There is also a splash pad near the soccer fields and pavilion.

Other Parks

Ceriani Park [B] - (Central and Jackson) If the kids are in need of a romp, try rolling down the grassy hills at Ceriani Park! There are also swings, a shaded picnic area and restrooms.

Kiddie Park [C] - (5th and Eagle) Aptly named, this park has perfect playground for little kids.

West Grand Elementary School [D] - (715 Kinsey Ave) During non-school hours this large, modern playground is open to the public, however there aren't any other amenities available.

Splash Spot

Splash Pad [E] - (208 N. 12th) You'll find a great place to cool down at West Grand High School, near the soccer fields and pavilion.

Kid-Friendly Eateries
(with something for adults too!)

Big Shooter Coffee [F] - 311 Park Avenue. (970) 724-3735
Ice cream for them, coffee for you!

Country Cupboard [G] - 104 N. 6th Street. (970) 724-9577
Breakfast all day, pizza, sandwiches and more in a home-style café.

Kremmling Mercantile Deli [H] - 101 Martin Way. (970) 724-8979
A great place to stop for a sandwich to go.

The Moose Café [I] - 115 Park Avenue. (970) 724-9987
"Home style cooking in a family atmosphere."

Things to do in Bad Weather

Heritage Park Museum J - *111 N. 4th Street.*
(970) 724-9390   www.grandcountymuseum.com/KremmlingMuseum.htm
This museum allows visitors a glimpse into the life of early ranchers in Grand County. The complex includes a 1906 DNW&P Train Depot, a livery, a barn, the old Kremmling jail, a fishing cabin and more. Open Fridays and Saturdays in the summer. $ (but kids under 6 are FREE)

Groceries/Supplies

Kremmling Mercantile K - *101 Martin Way.*
(970) 724-8979

More Info

Library: Kremmling Library L - *300 S. 8th Street.* (970) 724-9228   www.gcld.org

Hospital/Emergency Care: Kremmling Memorial Hospital - *214 S. 4th Street.*
(970) 724-3442   www.kremmlinghospital.org

Kremmling Area Chamber of Commerce & Visitor Center M - *203 Park Avenue.*
(877)573-6654 or (970)724-3472
www.kremmlingchamber.com/index.html

Other Fun Stuff

Wolford Mountain Reservoir N - The reservoir was completed in 1996 to provide water storage for the Colorado River Basin. It also provides countless recreational opportunities.

Wolford Campground - *27219 US-40.*
(866) 472-4943   www.wolfordcampground.com
Not just a camping stop. At the Wolford Campground you can also rent boats (pontoons, runabout boats, paddle boats, canoes and fishing boats), have a picnic or take a walk.

Green Mountain Reservoir O -
www.greenmountainreservoir.com
Swimming, wildlife viewing, camping, boating and fishing are all available at Green Mountain Reservoir.

Heeney Marina P - *0151 CR-1798*
(970)724-9441   www.heeneymarina.com
Drive around the reservoir to Heeney for a boat rental, snacks, water access and ice cream!

Directions

At the junction of CO-9 and US-40.

Kremmling

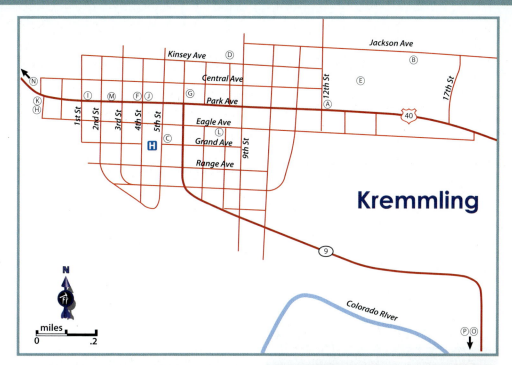

A. Veterans Memorial Park – 12th & Park Ave/US-40
B. Ceriani Park – Central & Jackson Avenues
C. Kiddie Park – 5th St, between Eagle and Grand
D. West Grand Elementary School – 715 Kinsey Ave
E. Splash Pad – 208 N. 12th
F. Big Shooter Coffee – 311 Park Avenue
G. Country Cupboard – 104 N. 6th Street
H. Kremmling Mercantile Deli – 101 Martin Way
I. The Moose Café – 115 Park Avenue
J. Heritage Park Museum – 111 N. 4th Street
K. Kremmling Mercantile – 101 Martin Way
L. Kremmling Library – 300 S. 8th Street
M. Chamber of Commerce & Visitor Center – 203 Park Avenue
N. Wolford Mountain Reservoir – 7 miles north of Kremmling on US-40
O. Green Mountain Reservoir – 17 miles south of Kremmling on CO-9
P. Heeney Marina – 0151 CR 1798

Leadville

"At the top of the Colorado Rockies"

Leadville is a mining boomtown with a colorful history. It is a National Historic Landmark full of Victorian architecture and an extensive mining district. The town also sits in a high mountain valley surrounded by the Sawatch and Mosquito Ranges, and is North American's highest incorporated city (10,430').

The Place to Go

Lake County Community Park [A] - (McWethy Dr and W. 6th) What a great surprise! While the park may be short on shade, the playground equipment is loads of fun, and the views couldn't be better. You'll also find lots of running around room, picnic tables and a public restroom.

Splash Spot

Turquoise Lake [B] - While the water will most likely be too cold for people to splash in, rocks are another story. There are many places to stop all around the lake.

Trails for Strollers & Little Folks

Mineral Belt Trail - www.mineralbelttrail.com
In Leadville they can boast that this is "the highest 12-mile, all-season, paved" trail. It loops around Leadville, through historic sites and the mining district. Those that conquer the entire loop travel through aspen groves, conifer forests, meadows, and sagebrush. No matter how far you travel, though, it's a great trail for a walk with unsurpassed views of the surrounding mountains. Easy access at the **Lake County Aquatic Center** [K] and at the **Lake County Public Library** [N].

Another Park

Kiddie Corral [C] - (9th and Poplar) Those in need of a quick and easy stop will think this is perfect. It's located just off US-24 at the north end of town. There is playground equipment, a sandbox, picnic tables and public restrooms.

Hayden Meadows Recreation Area [D] - (On US-24 south of town, just over the Arkansas River bridge) Here you'll find an excellent place for a picnic and a stroll along the nature trails. This is also a great spot for birding and fishing.

Kid-Friendly Eateries
(with something for adults too!)

Cookies With Altitude E - *717 ½ Harrison Avenue. (586) 596-0698*
They claim to be the highest bakery in the US, serving cookies, cakes, muffins and more.

Gringo's F - *102 Mountain View Drive. (719) 486-3227*
Family owned drive-thru that serves authentic Mexican fare, as well as typical American fare.

High Mountain Pies G - *115 W. 4th Street. (719) 486-5555*
Pizzas "crafted with love from the freshest of ingredients." Also a great shaded deck.

Manuelita's Mexican Restaurant H - *311 Harrison Avenue. (719)486-0292* manuelitasrestaurant.com
Another family owned business that serves a diverse selection of Mexican food.

Provin' Grounds Coffee and Bakery I - *508 Harrison Avenue. (719)486-0797*
Serving organic coffee and fresh baked goodies.

Tennessee Pass Café J - *222 Harrison Ave. (719) 486-8101   www.thetennesseepasscafe.com*
"Where good friends meet, and good people eat" for breakfast, lunch and dinner.

Things to do in Bad Weather

Lake County Aquatic Center K - *1000 West 6th Street. (719) 486-6986   www.lakecountyco.com*
A heated pool with diving boards, 2 slides and a large shallow play area...always a good bet in bad weather. $

Strikes-n-Spares L - *1717 N. Poplar. (719) 486-8905   www.strikes-n-spares.com*
If the kids are big enough, bowling is a great family activity, and an easy way to expend energy after traveling. $

Groceries/Supplies

Safeway M - *1900 US-24. (719) 486-0795*

More Info

Library: Lake County Public Library N - *1115 Harrison Avenue. (719) 486-0569* www.lakecountypubliclibrary.org

Hospital/Emergency Care: *St. Vincent Hospital - 822 W. 4th Street. (719) 486-0230* www.svghd.org

Visitor's Center: Leadville/Lake County Chamber of Commerce O - *809 Harrison Avenue. (719) 486-3900 OR (888) 532-3845* www.leadvilleusa.com

More info: www.visitleadvilleco.com

Other Fun Stuff

Leadville Colorado & Southern Railroad P - *326 E. 7th Street. (866) 386-3936 OR (719) 486-3936   www.leadville-train.com*
All aboard! This scenic 2½ hour train ride takes passengers 1,000 feet above the valley floor through rugged wilderness. $

National Mining Hall of Fame & Museum Q - *120 W. 9th Street. (719) 486-1229* www.mininghalloffame.org
The National Mining Hall of Fame & Museum is a tribute to the men and women who discovered and excavated our nation's natural resources. Exhibits include a model of a mountain mining town, complete with a railroad; 22 detailed wooden dioramas that portray mining history; artifacts from the Gold Rush; a mineral exhibit; and the popular Hard Rock Mine, a life-size model of an underground mine and equipment. $

Leadville National Fish Hatchery ᴿ -
2846 Highway 300. (719) 486-0189
www.fws.gov/leadville

This hatchery is the second oldest Federal hatchery in the U.S. It was established by Congress in 1889 to ensure sustainable populations of certain species of fish, and today provides trout to all areas of Colorado in need. Tours available, but please call ahead. FREE

Directions

From the south, use US-24.

From the north, travelers can use US-24 from Minturn, or CO-91 from Copper Mountain.

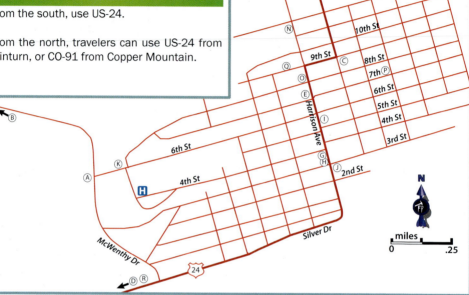

- A. Lake County Community Park – McWethy Drive & W. 6th
- B. Turquoise Lake
- C. Kiddie Corral – 9th & Poplar
- D. Hayden Meadows Recreation Area – US-24 south, past Crystal Lakes, just over the bridge where the highway crosses the Arkansas River; area is on the east side of the road
- E. Cookies with Altitude – 717 ½ Harrison Avenue
- F. Gringo's – 102 Mt View Drive
- G. High Mountain Pies -115 W. 4th Street
- H. Manuelita's – 311 Harrison Avenue
- I. Provin' Grounds Coffee & Bakery – 508 Harrison Avenue
- J. Tennessee Pass Café – 222 Harrison Avenue
- K. Lake County Aquatic Center – 1000 W. 6th Street
- L. Strikes-n-Spares – 1717 N. Poplar
- M. Safeway – 1900 US-24
- N. Lake County Public Library – 1115 Harrison Ave
- O. Visitor Center – 809 Harrison Avenue
- P. Leadville Colorado & Southern Railroad – 326 E. 7th Street
- Q. National Mining Museum – 120 W. 9th Street
- R. Leadville National Fish Hatchery – 2846 Hwy-300

Limon
The "Hub City" of the plains

This centrally located town on the eastern plains of Colorado has its roots in the railroad, beginning in 1888 when it was a work camp for the Union Pacific and Rock Island rail lines. And because of its location, it grew quickly, and continues to serve as a "Hub City."

The Place to Go

Limon Heritage Museum & Railroad Park [A] - (899 1st Street)
www.ourjourney.info/MyJourneyDestinations/LimonHeritageMuseum.asp

A stop here puts you in the heart of downtown Limon. If the kids need some play time, go to the Railroad Park at the west end of the complex. You'll find a playground, gardens, picnic tables, and paths to walk on.

Other Options

Doug Kissel Fishing Pond [B] - (on 1st St, just east of 4th Ave) This stocked, one acre pond is open to the public (and children under 16 can fish for without a license).

photos by Nathan Pulley

Limon Wetlands C - This 14 acre site is a short walk from the fishing pond and downtown via the *Limon Pedestrian/Bike Trail* E. It includes four types of wetlands and hosts a variety of wildlife, including migratory birds. If you have them handy, bring binoculars.

Splash Spot

Limon Municipal Pool D - (543 D Ave) A stop at the pool is a failsafe way to make little travelers happy. Big travelers, too! $

Trails for Strollers & Little Folks

Limon Pedestrian/Bike Trail E - If you need to stretch legs, park at the fishing pond and wander through the wildlife area on this gravel path. It will take you over a bridge and under the railroad tracks. Or, from the pond head in the other direction several blocks toward the center of town.

Kid-Friendly Eateries
(with something for adults too!)

Jenny's Mexican Food F - *599 Main Street.* (719) 775-9335
If you're looking for authentic, fresh Mexican food, stop here!

Ruby's G - *197 E Ave.* (719) 775-9565
Hearty homemade breakfasts, burgers, sandwiches and Mexican food.

South Side Food and Drink H - *680 Main Street.* (719) 775-9593
Home cooking in a family atmosphere. Try the green chili or steak.

Many *fast food* choices are also available along Main Street.

photos by Nathan Pulley

Limon

Things to do in Bad Weather

Limon Heritage Museum & Railroad Park [A] - *899 1st Street. (719) 775-8605*
www.ourjourney.info/MyJourneyDestinations/Limon-HeritageMuseum.asp

The Museum complex preserves the rich history of the high plains. Visit a historic train depot, a one-room schoolhouse and a Native American teepee; many more exhibits portray the history of ranches and railroads in the area. FREE

Groceries/Supplies

Limon Super Foods [I] - *858 Main Street. (719) 775-2282*

Loaf 'n Jug [J] - *707 Main Street. (719) 775-2522*

More Info

Library: Limon Memorial Library [K] - *205 E Avenue. (719) 775-2163*
lincolncounty.colibraries.org/Limon

Hospital/Emergency Care: *Plains Medical Center* - *820 1st Street. (719) 775-2367* plainsmedicalcenter.org/locations/limon.html

Limon Chamber of Commerce - *(719) 775-9418* www.limonchamber.com

Directions

The highways that intersect here are: I-70, US-24, US-40, US-287, and CO-71. Follow the business routes to downtown. This road becomes Main Street.

A. Limon Heritage Museum and Railroad Park – 899 1st Street
B. Doug Kissel Fishing Pond – 6 blocks east of the downtown traffic signal on First
C. Limon Wetlands – access using trails from the fishing pond
D. Limon Municipal Pool – 543 D Avenue
E. Limon Pedestrian/Bike Trail – access at the fishing pond
F. Jenny's Mexican Food – 599 Main Street
G. Ruby's – 197 E Avenue
H. South Side Food and Drink – 680 Main Street
I. Limon Super Foods – 858 Main Street
J. Loaf 'n Jug – 707 Main Street
K. Limon Memorial Library – 205 E Avenue

Montrose

"A base camp for deep adventure"

Located in a high desert, Montrose is surrounded by natural wonders: the San Juan Mountains to the south, the Uncompahgre Plateau to the west, Grand Mesa to the north, and Black Canyon National Park to the east.

The Place to Go

Baldridge Park [A] - (southwest side of town, on the Uncompahgre River) Tucked away from downtown on the west side of the city, along the Uncompahgre River, this park is an oasis. Not only will the kids love the playground, but the park is full of old growth trees that provide welcome shade in the summer. You'll also find restrooms, picnic tables, a duck pond, and access to the *Uncompahgre Riverway Trail*.

Other Parks

Buckley Park [B] - (N. Nevada Ave and N. 3rd St) With two large play structures and lots of shade, Buckley Park is a great stop easily accessible from Main Street/US-50. There are also open grassy areas, picnic tables and public restrooms.

Montrose Botanic Gardens [C] - (Niagra Rd and Pavilion Dr) These gardens are "demonstration gardens," which aim to educate the public about plants native to Colorado that will thrive in the high desert despite limited water. Thanks to the efforts of the Montrose Botanical Society, the Botanic Gardens showcase beautiful plants and flowers in a xeriscape setting. FREE www.montrosegardens.org

Splash Spot

Montrose Aquatics Center [D] - 25 Colorado Avenue. (970) 249-7705   www.montroserec.com
This center features indoor and outdoor pools, a "Slidewinder," the "Kermit" and the "Candyland Splashpad." $

Montrose

Trails for Strollers & Little Folks

Uncompaghre Riverway Trail
The long-term goal for this trail is to connect Montrose to Ouray to the south, and Delta to the north. For now, there are more than 5 miles of paved trail along the river, offering the perfect place for exploration. Best access at *Baldridge Park* [A] or at the *Ute Indian Museum* [J].

Kid-Friendly Eateries
(with something for adults too!)

Belly [E] - 309 E. Main Street. (970) 252-1488
A sophisticated and reasonably priced place to fill your belly.

Chili's [F] - 1431 Ogden Rd. (970) 249-7160
This chain offers a consistently good food in a family friendly atmosphere.

Jovis Coffee Roasters [G] - 242 E. Main Street (970) 252-0812 www.joviscoffee.com
The only all-organic coffee roaster in Montrose!

Smuggler's Brew Pub & Grille [H] - 1571 Ogden Rd. (970) 249-0919 www.smugglersbrew.com
Good food and good beer. What more could you need?

Things to do in Bad Weather

Climbing Tree Children's Museum [I] - 330 S. 8th St. (970) 240-8733 www.theclimbingtree.org
Inside the museum there are many interactive exhibits, to both educate and entertain. Visit a replica of the Space Shuttle, perform science experiments, build something in the construction zone, or dress up and perform a show. $

Ute Indian Museum [J] - 17253 Chipeta Rd. (along US-50, south of town) (970) 249-3098
www.coloradohistory.org/hist_sites/uteindian/ute_indian.htm
This museum offers one of the nation's most complete collections of Ute artifacts and sits on the site of Chief Ouray's homestead. Outside (if the weather breaks!) there is a shaded picnic area, walking paths, a memorial, and access to the *Uncompahgre Riverway Trail*. $

Groceries/Supplies

City Market [K] - 16400 S. Townsend Avenue. (970) 240-3236

Natural Grocers [L] - 3451 S. Rio Grande Ave. (970) 249-2724

Safeway [M] - 1329 S. Townsend Avenue. (970) 249-8822

More Info

Library: Montrose Regional Library District [N] - 320 S. 2nd Street. (970) 249-9656
http://www.montroselibrary.org/

Hospital/Emergency Care: *Montrose Memorial Hospital* - 800 S. Third Street. (970) 249-2211   www.montrosehospital.com

Visitor's Centers:
For those coming in from the east on US-50:
Chamber of Commerce [O] - 1519 E. Main Street. (970) 252-0505

For those coming in from the south on US-550:
Ute Indian Museum [J] - 17253 Chipeta Rd. (970) 249-3098   visitmontrose.com

Other Fun Stuff

Black Canyon of the Gunnison National Park [P] - (970) 249-1915 OR (970) 641-2337
www.nps.gov/blca
The canyon itself is 2,700 feet deep and 53 miles long. The narrow opening and sheer walls provide remarkable scenery. There are places for picnics, as well as hiking trails including the Rim Rock Nature Trail, a self-guided interpretive trail along the south rim of the canyon. $

Montrose

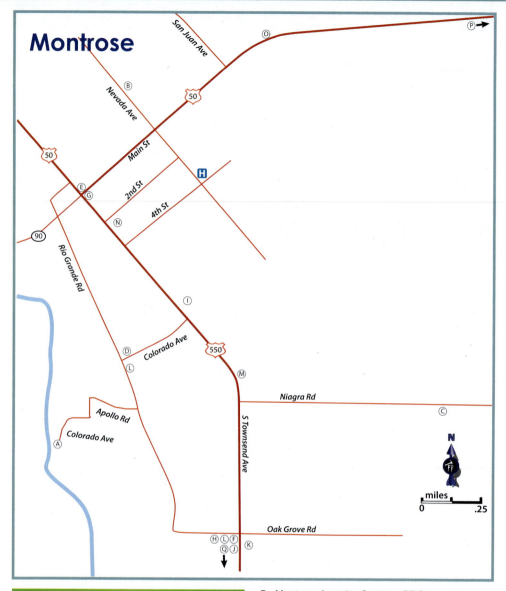

Directions

From the north or south, take US-550.
From the east, use US-50.

A. Baldridge Park – from south Rio Grande Ave, take Apollo Rd. west to Colorado Avenue; turn left
B. Buckley Park – N. Nevada Avenue & N. 3rd Street
C. Montrose Botanic Gardens – Niagra Rd. & Pavilion Drive (south of the Montrose Pavilion)
D. Montrose Aquatics Center – 25 Colorado Avenue
E. Belly – 309 E. Main Street
F. Chili's – 1431 Ogden Rd.
G. Jovis Coffee Roaster – 242 E. Main Street
H. Smuggler's Brew Pub & Grille – 1571 Ogden Rd.
I. Climbing Tree Children's Museum – 330 S. 8th St
J. Ute Indian Museum – 17253 Chipeta Rd.
K. City Market - 16400 S. Townsend Avenue
L. Natural Grocers - 3451 S. Rio Grande Avenue
M. Safeway - 1329 S. Townsend Avenue
N. Montrose Regional Library District – 320 2nd St
O. Chamber of Commerce – 1519 E. Main Street
P. Black Canyon of the Gunnison National Park – 15 miles east on US-50, north on CO-347

Ouray
"Switzerland of America"

When you see the towering, rugged peaks that surround Ouray, you'll understand why its nickname is "Switzerland of America." The town is surrounded on three sides by the mountains of the San Juans, many of which exceed 13,000 feet.

The Place to Go

Fellin Park [A] - (1220 Main St) Located at the hot springs complex, the playground here offers the perfect stopping spot. The kids will love the play equipment, and adults will love the view. There are also covered picnic tables, open fields, restrooms, and easy access to the *Uncompahgre River Walk*.

Splash Spot

Uncompahgre River - While the water will most likely be too cold or too fast to wade in, the river has endless rocks and sticks surrounding it, begging to be thrown into the water. Easiest access is along the *Uncompahgre River Walk*.

Box Canyon Waterfall and Park [B] - (US-550 south of Ouray) This box canyon is where Canyon Creek narrows and spews thousands of gallons of water a minute over the 285 foot fall. Visitors can view the falls from above or below, depending on how far everyone wants to walk. There are also interpretive trails for all abilities, as well as a visitor center with exhibits and more information. The area is also a great place for birding. $

Trails for Strollers & Little Folks

Uncompahgre River Walk -This two mile gravel loop along the river is great for strollers and little hikers. Along the way you can take in the view, have a picnic and find a spot to splash in the water. Access by crossing the bridge on the west side of *Fellin Park* [A], then follow the road north. The trail will be on your right after a quarter mile.

Kid-Friendly Eateries
(with something for adults too!)

Backstreet Bagel & Deli [C] - 636 Main Street. (970) 325-0550
Serving much more than just bagels, this deli is a great place for a lighter meal or one on the go.

Buen Tiempo Mexican Restaurant and Cantina [D] - 515 Main Street. (970) 325-4544
Unpretentious and friendly Mexican restaurant, complete with good margaritas and great views from the patio.

The Bistro at Billy Goat Gruff's [E] - 400 Main Street. (970) 325-4370   billygoatsouray.com
Burgers, salads, hearty entrées and even a "Little Goats" menu, all served with the best view in town.

Mouse's Chocolates & Coffee ᶠ - 520 Main Street. (970) 325-7285
www.mouseschocolates.com
Oh yeah, handmade chocolates and some of the best coffee in town.

Ouray Brewery ᴳ - 607 Main St. (970) 325-7388
Yes, beer. Plus good food and a great view to go with it.

Ouray Hot Springs Park ᴴ - 1220 Main Street. (970) 325-4813
Check out the snack bar here for burgers, dogs and sandwiches.

Things to do in Bad Weather

Ouray Hot Springs Park ᴴ - 1220 Main Street. (970) 325-7073   www.ourayhotsprings.com
As early as the 14th century the Ute Indians discovered the magic of the natural hot springs in Ouray. The pool was constructed in the 1920s and is listed on the National Historic Register. With three soaking pools of varying temperatures and great water slides (88°-105°), Ouray Hot Springs is a fun family activity. $

Bachelor-Syracuse Mine Tour ᴵ - 1222 CR 14 (12 miles north of Ouray, east on CR-14)
(970) 325-0220   www.bachelorsyracusemine.com
To better understand the history of Ouray, a tour of a real silver and gold mine is in order. Guides escort guests deep into the hill on a mine train to see ore veins, work areas and equipment used by miners. When you're done, the kids can try their hand at gold panning! $

Groceries/Supplies

Duckett's A.G. Market ᴶ - 621 Main Street. (970) 325-4397

More Info

Library: Ouray Public Library ᴷ - 320 6th Avenue. (970) 325-4616   ouray.colibraries.org

Hospital/Emergency Care: *Ouray Family Medicine* ᴸ - 824 Main Street. (970) 325-9900   www.ouraymed.com

Mountain Medical Center ᴹ - 295 Sherman Street, Ridgway. (970) 626-5123

Visitor's Center: Ouray Visitor Center ᴺ 1230 Main Street. (970) 325-4746
www.ouraycolorado.com

Other Fun Stuff

Ridgway State Park ᴼ - 28555 US-550, Ridgway. (970) 626-5822
This is a stop to make if you have some time because there is so much to do. There are picnic and playground areas, 14 miles of trails, loads of wildlife, great views and even a swim beach! $

Dennis Weaver Memorial Park ᴾ - (2 miles north of Ridgway off US-550) The 60-acre nature park and wildlife preserve on the Uncompahgre River is a serene and relatively unknown spot. There are miles of trails, breathtaking vistas and a riverside picnic area. FREE
www.dennisweaver.com/memorial_park/index.html

Ridgway Railroad Museum ᵠ - 150 Racecourse Rd., Ridgway. (970) 626-4373
www.ridgwayrailroadmuseum.org
This outdoor museum exhibits the history of the Rio Grande Southern, Silverton and D&RG narrow-gauge railroads. The indoor display includes more railroad artifacts, including photographs and models. FREE

Directions

Along US-550, in the Uncompahgre National Forest, just north of Red Mountain Pass.

Ouray

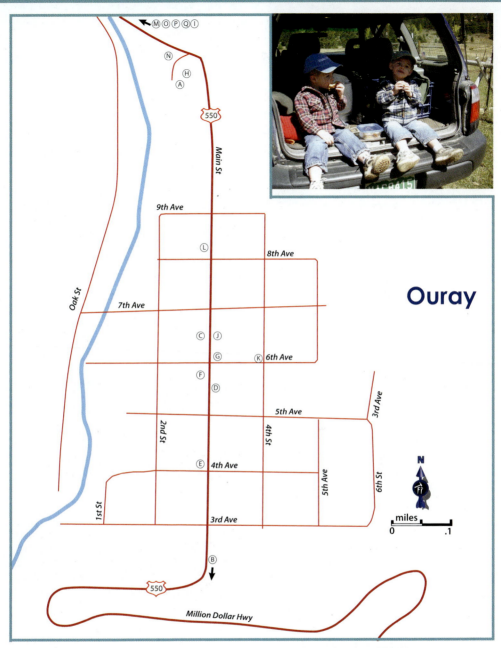

A. Fellin Park – 1220 Main Street
B. Box Canyon Waterfall and Park – follow US-550 south; take a right onto CR-361
C. Backstreet Bagel & Deli – 636 Main Street
D. Buen Tempo Mexican Restaurant – 515 Main St
E. The Bistro at Billy Goat Gruff's – 400 Main Street
F. Mouse's Chocolates & Coffee – 520 Main Street
G. Ouray Brewery – 607 Main Street
H. Ouray Hot Springs Park – 1220 Main Street
I. Bachelor-Syracuse Mine Tour – 1222 CR 14
J. Duckett's A.G. Market – 621 Main Street
K. Ouray Public Library – 320 6th Avenue
L. Ouray Family Medicine – 824 Main Street
M. Mountain Medical Center – 295 Sherman Street, Ridgway
N. Ouray Visitor Center – 1230 Main Street
O. Ridgway State Park – 6 miles north of Ridgway on US-550
P. Dennis Weaver Memorial Park – 2 miles north of Ridgway on US-550
Q. Ridgway Railroad Museum – 150 Racecourse Road, Ridgway

Pagosa Springs

"Refreshingly authentic"

Pagosa Springs gets its name from the Southwestern Ute word, "Pagosah," which means "healing waters." Visitors can enjoy not only the world-renown hot springs, but also panoramic mountain views and over 3 million acres of National Forest that surround the town.

The Place to Go

Town Park [A] - (Hermosa St and Hot Springs Blvd) This park is a good bet for "one-stop stopping." You'll find a playground, river access (and the water is even warm in many spots because of the hot springs!), the *River Walk Trail*, shade, picnic tables, and public restrooms. And, downtown is close enough that you don't have to get in the car again to find something to eat.

Another Park

River Center Park [B] - Drive around behind *The Malt Shoppe* [E] at the River Center, and you won't be disappointed. The park has loads of water access, short paths that crisscross around the ponds and down to the river, picnic tables, benches and spots for fishing.

Splash Spot

San Juan River - A stop in Pagosa Springs demands some time in the river. Because of the hot springs, the water is remarkably warm. If you have a tube, you can float through downtown! Easy access from *Town Park* [A] and along the *River Walk Trail*.

Trails for Strollers & Little Folks

Reservoir Hill Recreation Path-Spa Trailhead [C] - If you and your little hiker(s) want more of a hike than a stroll, try Reservoir Hill (no strollers here). At the trailhead there is a detailed map of the many choices of routes to take.

Pagosa Springs

Kid-Friendly Eateries
(with something for adults too!)

Kip's Grill & Cantina [D] - 121 Pagosa Street. (970) 264-3663   www.kipsgrill.com
"Pleasin' the people!" they say, with Mexican food and burgers too.

The Malt Shoppe [E] - 124 E. Pagosa Street, River Center. (970) 264-2784
A popular mom-and-pop place serving thick malts and juicy burgers.

Pagosa Baking Company [F] - 238 Pagosa Street. (970) 264-9348
www.pagosabakingcompany.com
Serving quiche, breakfast burritos, homemade baked goods, paninis and more.

Pagosa Brewing Company [G] - 118 N. Pagosa Blvd. (970) 731-2739
www.pagosabrewing.com
Award-winning beer for the big people, hand-crafted root beer for the little people, and "made from scratch" food.

River Pointe Coffee Café [H] - 445 San Juan Street (underneath the realty company, facing the river). (970) 264-3216
A cozy spot for coffee and a snack, right along the *River Walk Trail*.

Tequila's [I] - 439 San Juan Street (on the River Walk). (970) 264-9989   chatosytequilas.com
This family-owned business serves traditional Mexican food using old family recipes.

Things to do in Bad Weather

Healing Waters Resort and Spa [J] - 317 Hot Springs Boulevard. (800) 832-5523
www.pshotsprings.com
Play in the large pool heated by the natural mineral waters, or soak up the healing powers in one of the quieter hot tubs. This resort is also in close proximity to downtown restaurants and shops. $

River Walk Trail - Take a leisurely walk along the San Juan River on this trail. You'll have to hold the kids back, though, to keep them from getting in the water! The trail extends from *Town Park* [A] to 6th Street, and the town hopes to extend it in the future.

Pagosa Springs

Overlook Hot Springs Spa ᴷ - *432 Pagosa Street. (970) 264-404* www.overlookhotsprings.com Located in the heart of historic downtown, the highlight of a stop here is the rooftop tubs with views of the San Juan Mountains. They also have 5 indoor pools. $

Pagosa Game Space ᴸ - *535 San Juan Street/US-160. (970) 264-0522* This indoor game center has board games, Xbox, Wii, computer games, air hockey, concessions and more. $

The Springs Resort & Spa ᴹ - *165 Hot Springs Blvd. (800) 225-0934* www.pagosahotsprings.com This spa sits right on the banks of the San Juan River, and boasts 23 therapeutic mineral pools on various terraces all ranging in design, views and temperature. $

Groceries/Supplies

City Market ᴺ - *165 Country Center Drive. (970) 731-6000*

More Info

Library: Ruby M. Sisson ᴼ - *811 San Juan Street. (970) 264-2209* pagosa.colibraries.org

Hospital/Emergency Care: *Pagosa Mountain Hospital* - *95 S. Pagosa Blvd. (970) 731-3700* www.pagosamountainhospital.org

Pagosa Springs Area Chamber of Commerce & Visitor's Center ᴾ - *402 San Juan Street (access from Hot Springs Blvd., next to the Springs Resort). (970) 264-2360* www.pagosachamber.com

More Info: www.visitpagosasprings.com www.pagosa.com

Other Fun Stuff

Rocky Mountain Wildlife Park ᵠ - *4821 US-84. (970) 264-4515* www.rmwildlifepark.org Located a five miles east of Pagosa Springs on Hwy 84, this park is a great place to view native wildlife up close. Most of the animals at the facility are rescued, non-releasable animals, but are kept in environments closely mirroring their natural habitat. Their mission is not only to care for these animals, but to educate the public about species living in the San Juans. $

Directions

From the east or west, use US-160.

From the south, US-84 brings you to the east end of town.

Pagosa Springs

A. Town Park – Hermosa Street & Hot Springs Blvd.
B. River Center Park – east end of town on US-160, behind the River Center
C. Spa Trailhead – southern end of Park Street (yes, you must drive up the big hill)
D. Kip's Grill & Cantina – 121 Pagosa Street
E. The Malt Shoppe – 124 E. Pagosa Street
F. Pagosa Baking Co. – 238 Pagosa Street
G. Pagosa Brewing Company – 118 N. Pagosa Blvd.
H. River Pointe Coffee Café – 445 San Juan Street
I. Tequila's – 439 San Juan Street
J. Healing Waters Resort & Spa – 317 Hot Springs Blvd.
K. Overlook Hot Springs Spa – 432 Pagosa Street
L. Pagosa Game Space – 535 San Juan Street
M. The Springs Resort & Spa – 165 Hot Springs Blvd
N. City Market – 165 Country Center Drive
O. Ruby M. Sisson Library – 811 San Juan Street
P. Pagosa Springs Area Chamber of Commerce & Visitor's Center - 402 San Juan Street (but access from Hot Springs Blvd, next to the Springs Resort)
Q. Rocky Mountain Wildlife Park – 4821 US-84

Pueblo

Just east of the Rockies, Pueblo is one of Colorado's many bustling Front Range cities. Thanks to the completion of the Denver & Rio Grande Railroad in 1872 and the abundance of coal, Pueblo grew and became known as the Steel City. Since then it has continued to grow, and has evolved into a unique blend of culture, family, art, and farming.

The Place to Go

HARP (Historic Arkansas RiverWalk of Pueblo) [A] - 101 S. Union. (719) 595-0242
www.pueblohrap.com
This 32-acre waterfront park is in the heart of historic downtown Pueblo, and will truly surprise people that generally bypass this city. Along the paved walkway there are picnic tables, fountains to play in, restaurants nearby, and even places to rent paddle boats or take a waterway tour on an excursion boat or gondola. Information and restrooms available at the *Riverwalk Welcome Center* [P] at S. Union and the Riverwalk. The *Union Avenue Historic District* [B] is also nearby, with a variety of stores and restaurants.

Park

City Park [C] - (800 Goodnight Avenue) Yes, this park is way off the beaten path. But, if you have time and energy to expend, the drive is worth it because it's not just a park. There is a playground, picnic areas, walking paths, acres of open grassy areas, and public restrooms. But there is also the *Pueblo Zoo* [S], *City Park Pool* [E], stocked lakes, kiddie rides, a wooden carousel, and...a miniature train!

Splash Spots

Physicians Fountain [D] - (on the Riverwalk between Untion and Main) It will be as much fun for you to watch as it is for them to play in. Kids never know when the fountain might send a jet of water upward, and will squeal and run every time.

City Park Pool [E] - 800 Goodnight Avenue. (719) 553-2790
A great place for a cool down after some running around in the park. $

Pueblo 113

Trails for Strollers & Little Folks

Pueblo River Trail System
Pueblo has a remarkably intricate network of multi-use trails both within and outside city limits. One such improved trail runs parallel to the Arkansas River for 35 miles, from downtown to west of the city. Access points include where S. Main crosses the river west of downtown, and also on the north side of *City Park* ^C.

Kid-Friendly Eateries
(with something for adults too!)

Angelo's Pizza ^F - 105 East River Walk. (719) 544-8588
This pizza place located right on the Riverwalk; outside dining available.

The Daily Grind ^G - 209 South Union Avenue. (719) 561-8567
Not only do they serve great coffee, but good food for breakfast, lunch and dinner.

Shamrock Brewing Company ^H - 108 West 3rd Street. (719) 542-9974
www.shamrockbrewing.com
Shamrock Brewing Company is a unique blend of Irish pub, brewery and restaurant.

Things to do in Bad Weather

Buell Children's Museum ^J - 210 N Santa Fe Ave. (719) 295-7200   www.sdc-arts.org/bcc.html
This children's museum is touted as one of the best in the country. Come explore two floors of hands-on, interactive art, science and history exhibits. $

Pueblo Railway Museum ^K - 132 W. B Street (behind the Pueblo Union Depot). (719) 251-5024   www.pueblorailway.org
The museum is home to locomotives, freight cars, passenger cars and special purpose cars, many of which the kids will enjoy touching and climbing into in the rail yards. Inside the Heritage Center are railroad artifacts, and if that isn't enough, more than 20 real trains pass through the depot per day, allowing for some great train watching! FREE

Wireworks Coffeehouse ^I - 103 South Union Avenue (719) 543-3000
Also located on the Riverwalk, this eclectic coffeehouse serves coffee, breakfast all day, great vegetarian food and even creamy milkshakes.

Groceries/Supplies

King Soopers [L] - 102 West 29th Street. (719) 544-0390

Natural Grocers [M] - 101 West 29th Street. (719) 542-2411

Safeway [N] - 617 West 29th St. (719) 545-1095

More Info

Library: Rawlings Library [O] - 100 East Abriendo Avenue. (719) 562-5600 www.pueblolibrary.org

Hospital/Emergency Care: Parkview Medical Center - 400 West 16th Street. (719) 584-4000 www.parkviewmc.com

Visitor Information: Riverwalk Welcome Center [P] - 101 S. Union. (719) 595-0242 www.puebloharp.com

More Info: www.seepueblo.com

Other Fun Stuff

Lake Pueblo State Park [Q] - 640 Pueblo Reservoir Road. (719) 561-9320
http://parks.state.co.us/Parks/LakePueblo/Pages/LakePuebloStatePark.aspx
Only a few miles west of Pueblo, this state park is one of the best in the state for water sports, including fishing, boating and swimming. There are also many hiking trails and picnic spots. $

The Nature and Raptor Center of Pueblo [R] - 5200 Nature Center Road. (719) 549-2414 natureandraptor.org This non-profit educational, conservation and recreational facility is on the banks of the Arkansas River, in Rock Canyon. It is also a rehabilitation hospital for injured hawks, owls and eagles. On the grounds you'll find nature trails, access to the **Pueblo River Trail System**, a picnic area, playground and a café. $ (for parking)

Pueblo Zoo [S] - 3455 Nuckolls Avenue. (719) 561-1452   www.pueblozoo.org
Go wild at the zoo in **City Park** [C]! Explore the rain forest, learn about the American grasslands, take in the Serengeti Safari, or watch the northern river otters splash and play. The zoo's gardens are perfect for picnics. $

Royal Gorge Route Railroad [T] - 401 Water Street, Cañon City. (888) 724-5748
www.royalgorgeroute.com
If your travels take you west of Pueblo on US-50, stop in Cañon City for a ride on Colorado's premier train. The 2 hour, round-trip journey travels through the Royal Gorge with the white water of the Arkansas River tossing below you and the granite cliffs of the gorge towering above. $

Directions

From I-25 take exit 98b to 1st Street; head west on 1st and left onto South Union to get downtown.

Parking

There is plenty of street parking downtown, and also a large parking garage on S. Main between D Street and the Riverwalk.

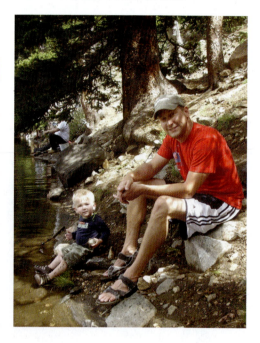

Pueblo

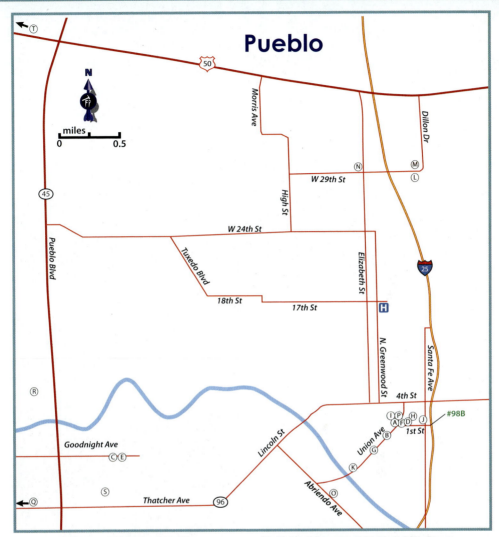

A. Historic Arkansas Riverwalk of Pueblo - 101 S. Union
B. Union Avenue Historic District – along Union Ave between Grand Avenue and B Street
C. City Park – 800 Goodnight Avenue
D. Physicians Fountain – on the Riverwalk between Union and Main
E. City Park Pool – 800 Goodnight Avenue
F. Angelo's Pizza – 105 East Riverwalk
G. The Daily Grind – 209 S. Union Avenue
H. Shamrock Brewing Company - 108 West 3rd Street
I. Wireworks Coffeehouse - 103 South Union Avenue
J. Buell Children's Museum - 210 N Santa Fe Avenue
K. Pueblo Railway Museum - 132 W. B Street
L. King Soopers - 102 West 29th Street
M. Natural Grocers - 101 West 29th Street
N. Safeway - 617 West 29th Street
O. Rawlings Library - 100 East Abriendo Ave
P. Riverwalk Welcome Center – 101 S. Union
Q. Lake Pueblo State Park - 640 Pueblo Reservoir Rd.
R. The Nature and Raptor Center of Pueblo - 5200 Nature Center Road
S. Pueblo Zoo - 3455 Nuckolls Ave.
T. Royal Gorge Route Railroad - Sante Fe Depot, 401 Water Street, Cañon City

Salida

"Heart of the Rockies"

"Headwaters of Adventure"

"Now This is Colorado"

There truly is a lot going on in Salida. For starters, it sits on the Arkansas River, making it a playground for boaters. The town is also surrounded by the Collegiate Peaks, including 13 mountains over 14,000 feet, allowing for endless opportunities for adventure. And, Salida has also evolved into a renowned art community.

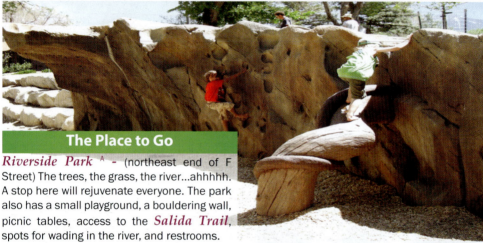

The Place to Go

Riverside Park [A] - (northeast end of F Street) The trees, the grass, the river...ahhhhh. A stop here will rejuvenate everyone. The park also has a small playground, a bouldering wall, picnic tables, access to the *Salida Trail*, spots for wading in the river, and restrooms.

Another Park

Alpine Park [B] - (4th and F Street) For those not interested in going downtown, Alpine Park is a great alternative. It also has large shade trees and open grassy areas. There are two playground structures, picnic tables and restrooms as well.

Splash Spot

Arkansas River - The river runs right by downtown. Take a stroll along the *Salida Trail* and you'll be guaranteed to find many places to enjoy the water. Watch for high water levels in the spring and early summer!

Trails for Strollers & Little Folks

Salida Trail - This trail is part of the Rails-to-Trails effort, and used to be the old narrow gauge railroad track that led into the mountains. It is an 8 mile improved trail that runs, in part, along the Arkansas River. Easiest access at *Riverside Park* [A].

Salida

Kid-Friendly Eateries
(with something for adults too!)

Amícas Pizza & Microbrewery C - *136 E. 2nd Street. (719) 539-5219*
Pizza and beer! And even kid-sized pies for little travelers.

Country Bounty D - *413 W. US-50. (719) 539-3546   www.thecountrybounty.com*
This family-style restaurant serves breakfast, lunch and dinner, and also bakes their own pastries, pies and cobblers.

Fiesta Mexicana E - *1220 US-50. (719) 539-5203*
A great family Mexican restaurant with an extensive menu. And, in good weather, the large outdoor patio is open.

First Street Café F - *137 E. First Street. (719) 539-4759   www.firststreetcafesalida.com*
First Street Café, right downtown, is a locals' spot, and serves burgers, sandwiches, Mexican food and more. They even have a wide-ranging kids' menu.

Moonlight Pizza G - *242 F Street. (719) 539-4277   www.moonlightpizza.biz*
Moonlight Pizza was voted the Best Pizza in Salida, and has also received votes for the Best Margarita and the Best Patio.

The Salida Cafe and Roastery H - *300 W Sackett Ave. (719) 539-4261   www.salidacafe.com*
A combo coffee shop and bakery, the Salida Cafe has not only organic coffee, but counter service for their full breakfast, lunch and dinner menus. And, the food can be enjoyed outside on the deck overlooking the Arkansas.

Things to do in Bad Weather

Salida Hot Springs Pool I - *410 W. US-50. (719) 539-6738   www.salidapool.com*
This hot springs facility was a WPA project in 1937, and employed 200 men to lay the original 8 miles of pipes to bring the springs water from its source. The pool and buildings have been updated several times, and today offer a relaxing place for soaking and recreating. $

Groceries/Supplies

Safeway J - *232 G Street. (719) 539-3513*

More Info

Library: Salida Regional Library K - *405 E Street. (719) 539-4826*
salida.colibraries.org

Hospital/Emergency Care: *Heart of the Rockies Regional Medical Center* - *1000 Rush Drive. (719) 530-2200*
www.hrrmc.com

Chamber of Commerce L - *406 W. US-50. (719) 539-2068   www.salidachamber.org*

More info: www.salida.com

Other Fun Stuff

Mt. Shavano State Fish Hatchery M - *7725 CR 154. (719) 539-6877*
wildlife.state.co.us/Education/TeacherResources/Hatcheries.ht
This hatchery is one of the largest in the state, specializing in trout of all varieties. There is also a visitor center with wildlife exhibits, and guided tours. During non-summer months, call ahead for a tour. FREE

Directions

From the north, use US-285 south, then CO-291 to bring you into town.

From the east or west, US-50 brings travelers just south of downtown.

And from the south, take US-285 north to US-50 east.

Salida

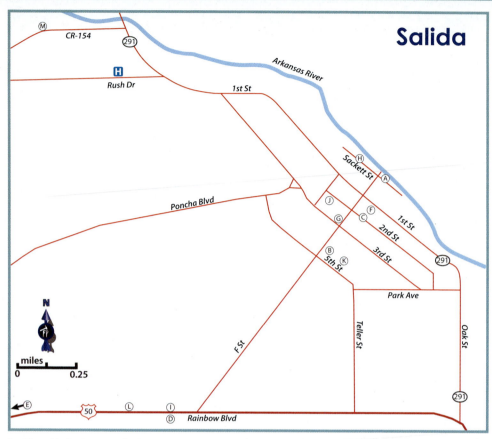

A. Riverside Park – end of F Street, at the bridge
B. Alpine Park – 4th & F Streets
C. Amícas Pizza & Microbrewery - 136 E. 2nd Street
D. Country Bounty - 413 W. US-50
E. Fiesta Mexicana - 1220 US-50
F. First Street Café - 137 E. First Street
G. Moonlight Pizza - 242 F Street
H. Salida Cafe and Roastery - 300 W Sackett Ave
I. Salida Hot Springs Pool - 410 W. US-50
J. Safeway – 232 G Street
K. Salida Regional Library – 405 E Street
L. Chamber of Commerce - 406 W. US-50
M. Mt. Shavano State Fish Hatchery – 7725 CR 154

Silverthorne

Folks often think of outlet stores when they pass through Silverthorne. But with the Continental Divide on one side, the Gore Range on the other, and the Blue River running through the middle of town, Silverthorne has a whole lot more to offer.

The Place to Go

Rainbow Park [A] - (430 Rainbow Dr) This is the park you always wished you knew about, and is easily one of the top 5 playgrounds in Colorado. There are several large play structures, two are three stories high! There are also picnic shelters, open fields and public restrooms.

Another Park

Trent Park [B] - (Willowbrook Rd & CO-9) This small, neighborhood park is an easy stop if you're traveling CO-9. There's a playground, picnic shelter and a small fishing pond.

Splash Spots

North Pond Park [C] - (Hamilton Creek Rd and CO-9) Yes, there's a pond here, as well as a wetland area that's home to nesting osprey. You'll also find a pavilion, picnic shelter, a short walking trail, two fishing docks and restrooms.

Blue River - Take a walk along the *Blue River Trail* and you'll easily find many spots to access the water for toe dipping or rock tossing. Be wary of water levels, especially in the spring and early summer.

Silverthorne

Trails for Strollers & Little Folks

Blue River Trail - This trail connects to others in Summit County. Access at *North Pond Park* C or at Willow Grove Open Space (at the north end of Mesa Drive).

Kid-Friendly Eateries
(with something for adults too!)

Chipotle D - 247 Rainbow Drive. (970) 468-0671
Fast and tasty burritos, burrito bowls and salads.

Mountain Lyon Café E -381 Blue River Parkway. (970) 262-6229
A good place to go for healthy foods and vegetarian specials.

Old Chicago F - 560 Silverthorne Lane. (970) 468-2882
Pizza, pizza, pizza and beer, beer, beer.

Red Buffalo Coffee and Tea G - 358 Blue River Parkway. (970) 468-4959
www.cupinthecorner.com
Serving specialty teas and coffees with a view.

Smiling Moose Deli H - 273 Summit Place. (970) 513-1414   www.smilingmoosedeli.com
Hot and cold sandwiches, wraps, soups and more.

Things to do in Bad Weather

Silverthorn Recreation Center I - 430 Rainbow Drive. (970) 262-7370
The swimming area has four pools and 3 water slides, and temperatures range form 90-92°. Visitors can also play in the gym, run on the track, drop in on a fitness class or use the weight room.

Groceries/Supplies

City Market J - 300 Dillon Ridge Road, Dillon. (970) 468-236

Target K - 715 Blue River Parkway. (970) 468-2268

More Info

Library: Summit County Library – North Branch L - 651 Center Circle. (970) 468-5887   www.co.summit.co.us/library

Hospital/Emergency Care: *St. Anthony's Summit Medical Center* - 340 Peak 1 Drive, Frisco. (970) 668-3300
www.summitmedicalcenter.org

High Country Health Care M - 265 Tanglewood Lane. (970) 468-1003
www.highcountryhealth.com/offices/silverthornefp.htm

Summit Information Center N - 246 Rainbow Drive (in the Green Village). (970) 468-5780 (information on Summit County and the outlets)

More information:
Town of Silverthorne. (970) 262-7300
www.silverthorne.org

Other Fun Stuff

Dillon Marina O - 300 Marina Drive, Dillon. (970) 468-5100   www.dillonmarina.com
Drive up to Dillon for a full-service marina on the Dillon Reservoir. BYOB (boat, that is), or rent one, for a day on the water. Explore the lake, fish, or just bask in the sun.

Outlets at Silverthorne P - (970) 468-5780
www.outletsatsilverthorne.com
A little shopping anyone? The choices are endless, including outlets for kids' clothing.

Directions

From I-70, use Exit 205 and head north.

From the north CO-9 will bring you into town.

If you're coming from the south, use US-6.

Silverthorne

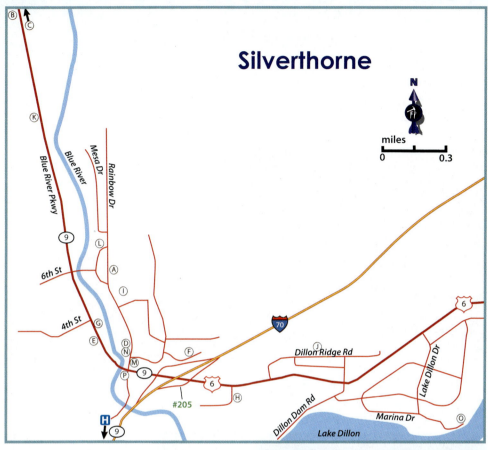

A. Rainbow Park – 430 Rainbow Drive
B. Trent Park – Willowbrook Rd. & CO-9
C. North Pond Park – Hamilton Creek Rd. & CO-9
D. Chipotle – 247 Rainbow Drive
E. Mountain Lyon Café – 381 Blue River Parkway
F. Old Chicago – 560 Silverthorne Lane
G. Red Buffalo Coffee & Tea – 358 Blue River Parkway
H. Smiling Moose Deli – 273 Summit Place
I. Silverthorne Recreation Center – 430 Rainbow Dr
J. City Market – 300 Dillon Ridge Road, Dillon
K. Target – 715 Blue River Parkway
L. Summit County Library – North Branch - 651 Center Circle
M. High Country Health Care – 265 Tanglewood Lane
N. Summit Information Center - 246 Rainbow Drive (in the Green Village)
O. Dillon Marina – 300 Marina Drive
P. Outlets at Silverthorne

Steamboat
"Ski Town USA"

Steamboat Springs, also known as "The Boat," lies in the upper valley of the Yampa River, west of the Continental Divide. It earned its name from fur trappers in the 1860s who said that Steamboat Spring, one of the more than 150 geothermal hot springs in the area, sounded like a steamboat.

The Place to Go

West Lincoln Park [A] - (13th St & Lincoln Ave) For something a little different, play on the steamboat-shaped playground equipment and visit Steamboat Spring, the spring from which the town eventually got its name. In addition, West Lincoln Park is right on the river and the ***Yampa River Core Trail***, is close to downtown, plus has picnic tables, restrooms and shade.

Other Parks

Little Toots Park [B] - (12th and Yampa) While in many ways this is a typical town park, it is a great place to get out of the car and re-group. Not only is there a playground, but you'll also find picnic tables, a gazebo, shade, and easy access to the ***Core Trail*** and the river. Also within a stone's throw are the library and downtown shops and restaurants.

Emerald Park [C] - (south end of Pamela Lane) Emerald Park is the place to go if you want to avoid crowds. Because, unless there are ball games going on, your kids will probably have the playground to themselves. There are also restrooms here, picnic tables, open fields and access to the ***Yampa River Core Trail***.

Splash Spot

Dr. Rich Weiss Park ^D - (3rd St and Lincoln Ave) Go here! Go here! Go here! This spot is not readily visible, but once you find it you'll go back again and again. Along the Yampa River, this park is a place where the hot springs warm the water, and past visitors have created small pools with the river rocks. In addition, there are lovely spots for a picnic, access to the *Yampa River Core Trail*, and even public restrooms.

Trails for Strollers & Little Folks

Fish Creek Falls ^E - This is a popular and sometimes crowded trail, but also good for kids because the hike is only ¼ mile to the first waterfall. The trail continues for many miles, depending on your interests. No strollers. $ (for parking)

Spring Creek Trail (at Spring Creek Park) ^F - From where you park at East Maple St and Amethyst St, walk up CR-34 to Spring Creek Park. Eventually the trail becomes single track, following the creek up the canyon.

Yampa River Core Trail - This seven mile, paved, multi-use path follows the Yampa River through town. It's perfect for a stroll or to use as a means to travel across town. Easy access at *Dr. Rich Weiss Park* ^D, at *Little Toots Park* ^B or *West Lincoln Park* ^A.

Kid-Friendly Eateries
(with something for adults too!)

Backcountry Provisions G - 635 Lincoln (Old Town Square). (970) 879-3617
www.backcountryprovisions.com
A deli to delight everyone. Plan to spend some time picking the perfect sandwich...there are a lot of choices.

Creekside Café & Grill H - 131 11th Street. (970) 879-4925   www.creekside-cafe.com
Serving breakfast and lunch daily, locals and visitors return regularly for the "legendary eggs benedict" and other delicious entrees.

Fuzziwig's Candy Factory I - 845 Lincoln Avenue. (970) 879-6194
www.sweetsfromheaven.com
Choices to suit every sweet-tooth.

Mambo Italiano J - 521 Lincoln Avenue. (970) 870-0500
Award-winning Italian cuisine in a happenin' atmosphere.

Off the Beaten Path K - 68 9th Street. (970) 879-6830 or (800) 898-6830
www.steamboatbooks.com
"Good books, good coffee, good friends."

Steamboat Smokehouse L - 912 Lincoln Ave. (970) 879-7427
www.steamboatsmokehouse.com
Lookin' for bbq? Stop here for an affordable, finger-lickin' good meal.

Winona's M - 617 Lincoln Ave. (970) 879-2483
This is the place to go for breakfast in Steamboat. Don't be surprised if there's a wait, but don't leave. It's worth it.

Things to do in Bad Weather

Old Town Hot Springs N - 136 Lincoln Ave. (970) 879-1828   steamboathotsprings.org
The pools at Old Town Hot Springs have been a central part of the town of Steamboat Springs for over 100 years. Before that, the springs were a bathing and gathering place for the Ute Indians. Today the eight hot spring fed pools include two waterslides, a lap pool and a kiddie pool. Temperatures range between 98-103°. $

Groceries/Supplies

City Market O - 1825 Central Park Drive. (970) 879-3290

Safeway P - 37500 US-40   (970) 879-3766

More Info

Bud Werner Memorial Library Q - 1289 Lincoln Avenue. (970) 879-0240
www.steamboatlibrary.org

Hospital/Emergency Care: **Yampa Valley Medical Center** - 1024 Central Park Drive. (970) 879-1322   www.yvmc.org

Steamboat Springs Chamber Resort Association R - Visitor Information Center 125 Anglers Drive.   (970) 879-0880
www.steamboat-chamber.com

Other Fun Stuff

Howelsen Hill Recreation Area S - (northwest end of Howelson Parkway) Howelsen Park literally has everything (except a fishing pond): **Core Trail** access, horseback riding, hiking, picnic tables, playground, open fields, an alpine slide and restrooms.

Howelsen Hill Alpine Slide - 645 Howelsen Parkway (at the **Howelsen Hill Recreation Area** S). (970) 819-8010
www.steamboatalpineslide.com
Fun for all of you! The adventure starts on the chairlift ride to the top of Howelsen Hill. Then, using a "sled" given to you at the top, whiz down the 2,400' cement track as it bends and curves, and you laugh and scream.

Steamboat Springs 125

Steamboat Gondola ^T - *At the base of Mt. Werner in Gondola Square. (970) 879-6111*
The kids will love the ride and you'll love the views from the 8-passenger gondola. At the top enjoy the wildflowers, take a hike or eat a meal at the Sun Deck.

Steamboat Lake State Park ^U - *61105 CR 129, Clark. (970) 879-3922*
http://parks.state.co.us/Parks/SteamboatLake/Pages/SteamboatLakeHome.aspx
If you go, you'll to want to stay the day. There are plenty of hiking trails for all abilities, a swim beach, boats to rent, picnic tables, and fishing spots. $

Steamboat Lake Marina ^V - *61450 County Road 62, Clark. (970) 879-7019*
www.steamboatlakemarina.com
You can rent boats at the marina (pontoon boats, kayaks, canoes, paddleboats, fishing boat rentals); stock up on supplies and groceries; or rent a camper cabin. $

Strawberry Park Hot Springs ^W - *44200 CR-36. (970) 879-0342*
www.strawberryhotsprings.com
Take a soak in the mineral springs of Hot Springs Creek. Strawberry Park seeks to maintain the natural beauty of the area while making the pools accessible to all. $

Yampa River Botanic Park ^X - (south part of town, near *Emerald Park* ^C) This botanic park features the plants, trees and shrubs native to the area. In addition, its location by the river also makes it a safe nesting place for birds. FREE

Directions

Steamboat Springs is along US-40, west of Rabbit Ears Pass.

Parking

Ample free parking street-side or in marked public lots.

126 Steamboat Springs

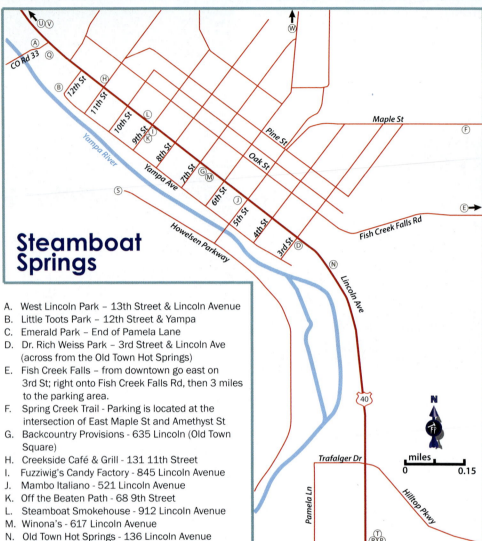

Steamboat Springs

A. West Lincoln Park – 13th Street & Lincoln Avenue
B. Little Toots Park – 12th Street & Yampa
C. Emerald Park – End of Pamela Lane
D. Dr. Rich Weiss Park – 3rd Street & Lincoln Ave (across from the Old Town Hot Springs)
E. Fish Creek Falls – from downtown go east on 3rd St; right onto Fish Creek Falls Rd, then 3 miles to the parking area.
F. Spring Creek Trail - Parking is located at the intersection of East Maple St and Amethyst St
G. Backcountry Provisions - 635 Lincoln (Old Town Square)
H. Creekside Café & Grill - 131 11th Street
I. Fuzziwig's Candy Factory - 845 Lincoln Avenue
J. Mambo Italiano - 521 Lincoln Avenue
K. Off the Beaten Path - 68 9th Street
L. Steamboat Smokehouse - 912 Lincoln Avenue
M. Winona's - 617 Lincoln Avenue
N. Old Town Hot Springs - 136 Lincoln Avenue
O. City Market – 1825 Central Park Drive
P. Safeway – 37500 US-40
Q. Bud Werner Memorial Library - 1289 Lincoln Ave
R. Steamboat Springs Chamber Resort Association - 125 Anglers Drive (south end of town, off US-40)
S. Howelsen Hill Recreation Area – Northwest end of Howelsen Parkway
T. Steamboat Gondola – Base of Mt. Werner in Gondola Square
U. Steamboat Lake State Park - 61105 CR 129, Clark
V. Steamboat Lake Marina - 61450 County Road 62, Clark
W. Strawberry Park Hot Springs - 44200 CR-36
X. Yampa River Botanic Park – from US-40 take Trafalger Drive to Pamela Lane; parking at the far end of the lot.

Telluride

The soaring 13,000-foot peaks of the San Juan Mountains that surround the town of Telluride first provided protection to the Ute Indians who traveled into the valley. Later, those same mountains spurred the mining boom when gold and silver were discovered, while the waterfalls led to the discovery of alternating current at the turn of the century.

The Place to Go

Town Park [A] - (West end of Colorado Ave) The Town Park in Telluride has a little bit of everything. Start at the *Imagination Station Playground* [B] for hours of climbing, swinging, running and jumping, or for smaller climbers try the Toddler Playground near the pond. After that the kids can catch a trout at the Kid's Fishing Pond (and rods are available to borrow at no cost at the Information Center in the park), and then take a walk along the river on the *San Miguel River Trail*. In Town Park there are also picnic tables, benches, paths and public restrooms.

Splash Spots

San Miguel River - So many splash spots, so little time. The river runs the length of town, and a walk on the *San Miguel River Trail* will afford many places to wade or toss rocks.

Telluride Community Pool [C] - *In Town Park.* (970) 728-2173
Another great aspect of *Town Park* [A] is the pool. For some water time, drop in at the outdoor pool. $

Trails for Strollers & Little Folks

San Miguel River Trail - This gravel, multi-use path runs along the San Miguel River the length of town. It's the perfect trail for a family walk and to hunt for splash spots. Access from any street in town that extends to the river, or at *Town Park* A.

Bear Creek Trail D - The Bear Creek Preserve includes more than 300 acres of land adjacent to *Town Park* A. To access the trail, follow Pine Street south to its end. The hike is 2.5 miles one way to the falls, but even if you don't go that far, the trail itself provides the opportunity for exploration and sight-seeing.

Kid-Friendly Eateries
(with something for adults too!)

Oak E - 250 San Juan Avenue. (970) 728-3985
Oak is the locals' place to go for great barbeque and a beer.

Maggie's Bakery & Café F - 217 E. Colorado Avenue. (970) 728-3334
Hearty, fresh breakfasts and lunches.

Smuggler's Brew Pub and Grille G - 225 S. Pine Street. (970) 728-0919
www.smugglersbrew.com
Many award-winning brews and lagers, and a full menu with something for everyone.

Steaming Bean Coffee Company H - 221 W. Colorado Avenue. (970) 369-5575
www.steamingbeantelluride.com
They serve not only gourmet coffee, but cocktails as well!

The Sweet Life I - 115 W. Colorado Avenue. (970) 728-8789   www.thesweetlifeinc.com
Serving the best ice cream and candy in town in a '50s style parlor.

Things to do in Bad Weather

Telluride Historical Museum J - 201 W. Gregory. (970) 728-3344
www.telluridemuseum.org
The Telluride Historical Museum allows visitors to travel back in time to experience the trials of mining life; to study early mining technology; to see how the arrival of the Rio Grande Southern Railroad changed the course of the town; to discover the creativity and ingenuity of the early settlers that allowed them to prosper in the rugged, remote town; and to explore more of the rich history and spirit of Telluride. $

Groceries/Supplies

Clark's Market K - 700 West Colorado Avenue. (970) 728-3124   www.clarksmarket.com

The Village Market L - 157 South Fir Street (970) 728-4566

More Info

Library: Wilkinson Public Library M - 100 W. Pacific Avenue. (970) 728-4519

Hospital/Emergency Care: *Telluride Medical Center* N - 500 West Pacific Avenue. (970) 728-3848   tellmed.org

Telluride Tourism Board
www.visittelluride.com

Telluride Visitor Center O - 700 W. Colorado Avenue (above Clark's Market). (888) 355-8743

More Info: www.telluride.com/

Other Fun Stuff

Gondola P - Station Telluride – Oak Street
The gondola in Telluride is the only one of its kind in North America: it serves as a primary transportation system between Telluride and the Mountain Village and is free to all passengers. The 2.5 mile ride takes about 15 minutes and is operated on wind power. At the top you can take a hike, visit the Mountain Village or simply take in the scenery. FREE

Telluride

Directions

There's only one paved road in and out of Telluride: From CO-145, head east, following signs, on Colorado Avenue (which is also marked CO-145).

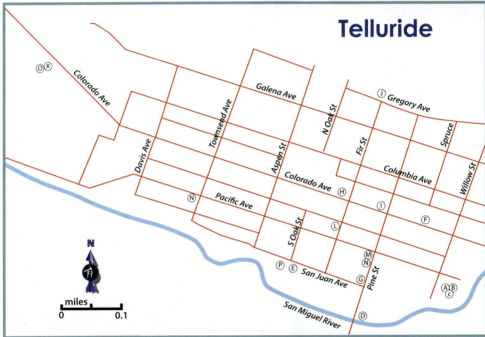

A. Town Park – west end of Colorado Avenue
B. Imagination Station Playground – next to the Hanley Rink Pavilion
C. Telluride Community Pool – in Town Park
D. Bear Creek Trail – access at south end of Pine St
E. Oak – 250 San Juan Avenue
F. Maggie's Bakery & Café -217 E. Colorado Avenue
G. Smuggler's Brew Pub and Grille - 225 S. Pine St
H. Steaming Bean Coffee Company - 221 W. Colorado Avenue
I. The Sweet Life - 115 W. Colorado Avenue
J. Telluride Historical Museum - 201 W. Gregory
K. Clark's Market - 700 West Colorado Avenue
L. The Village Market - 157 South Fir Street
M. Wilkinson Public Library - 100 W. Pacific Ave
N. Telluride Medical Center - 500 West Pacific Ave
O. Telluride Visitor Center - 700 W. Colorado Avenue (above Clark's Market)
P. Gondola – Station Telluride – Oak Street

Vail

The Gore Valley was first home to the Ute Indians, until they were driven out by fortune seekers in the late 1800s. After resources were depleted and mines abandoned, sheep ranchers stayed. During World War II the Army's Tenth Mountain Division used the area for backcountry survival training. Finally, in the mid-1950s the vision of Vail as a mountain ski community took shape and the town was incorporated in 1966.

The Place to Go

Vail Village [A] - This is one-stop stopping at its best. Park at the *Vail Village Parking* [V], walk west across the covered bridge, and everything will be at your fingertips.

Parks

Betty Ford Alpine Gardens [B] - (530 S Frontage Rd) www.bettyfordalpinegardens.org At 8,200', these gardens are the world's highest botanic gardens. Stroll along an intricate series of paved and gravel paths to enjoy high alpine plants and flowers native to the Rocky Mountain Region. FREE

Red Sandstone Park [C] - This park has a custom playground, access to the North Recreation Path, picnic tables, and restrooms.

Ford Park [E] - (530 S Frontage Rd) Before or after visiting the gardens, the kids will enjoy playing the playground in Ford Park. You'll also find picnic tables and shelters, access to the *Gore Valley Trail*, restrooms, splash spots in the river and the world famous Gerald R. Ford Amphitheatre. This is also the easiest park to access by car.

Trails for Strollers & Little Folks

Gore Valley Trail - This trail meanders through the valley, connecting parks, recreation facilities and Vail's core village areas. It also connects to the Eagle Valley Trail to the west, and to the Vail Pass trail to the east. Access at *Vail Village Parking* [V], *Lionshead Parking* [W], or *Ford Park* [E].

Pirate Ship Park [D] - (at the top of Bridge St) Brush up on your pirate-lingo and set off on an adventure at this custom playground. You might not need to do anything else! But, if you do, Pirate Park also has picnic tables, access to the rec path and the river, and is within walking distance of restaurants and shops in *Vail Village* [A]. Closest parking is at *Vail Village Parking* [V].

Vail   131

photos by Nathan Pulley

Village Streamwalk - This unpaved, short, pedestrian-only trail follows the banks of Gore Creek. It's the perfect "hike" to find splash spots. It begins at the covered bridge in *Vail Village* [A] and ends in *Ford Park* [E].

Splash Spots

Children's Fountain [F] - (E. Gore Creek Dr) In the heart of *Vail Village* [A], the fountain provides a great spot to cool down. In addition, there are many other fountains and water features throughout Vail Village.

Vail

Gore Creek - Follow any rec path, or the *Village Streamwalk*, and you'll find numerous spots in which to wade and play.

Kid-Friendly Eateries
(with something for adults too!)

Joe's Famous Deli [G] - 288 Bridge Street (Vail Village). (970) 479-7580
Joe's serves breakfast, as well as grilled and deli sandwiches for lunch and dinner. Homemade ice cream, too!

La Cantina [H] - 241 S. Frontage Road. (at the Vail Village Parking Structure) (970) 476-7661
Mexican and American food, all made from scratch.

Loaded Joe's [I] -227 Bridge Street (Vail Village). (970) 479-2883
Fantastic coffee and smoothies, and a simple menu of food items.

Moe's Original Bar-B-Que [J] - 616 W. Lionshead Circle. (970) 479-7888
www.moesoriginalbbq.com
This restaurant features southern-style eats, including great barbeque.

Red Lion Restaurant [K] - 304 Bridge St. (Vail Village). (970) 476-7676   www.theredlion.com
Casual pub downtown serving burgers, salads, soups, chili, bbq, and a kids' menu.

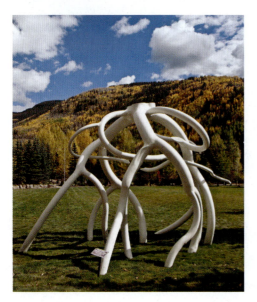

Things to do in Bad Weather

Imagination Station [L] - 395 East Lionshead Circle. (970) 479-2292
http://www.vailrec.com/facilities.cfm
Don't let bad weather bring you down...Vail's Imagination Station is a wondrous place for children, filled with hands-on activities. In addition, potty-trained children three and older are eligible for a three hour drop-off program. $

Groceries/Supplies

City Market [M] - 2109 N Frontage Road. (970) 476-1017

Safeway [N] - 2131 N Frontage Road. (970) 476-3561

More Info

Library: Vail Public Library [O] - 292 West Meadow Drive. (970) 479-2185

Hospital/Emergency Care: *Vail Valley Medical Center* [P] - 181 W. Meadow Drive. (970) 476-2451   www.vvmc.com

Visitor's Center - *Vail Visitor Information Center* [Q] - 241 S. Frontage Rd. (at the Vail Village Parking Structure). (970) 476-4790

Lionshead Information Center [R] - 395 S. Frontage Rd. (at the Lionshead Parking Structure) (970) 476-4941   www.visitvailvalley.com

More Info: www.vail.com
summer.vail.com/summer

Other Fun Stuff

Eagle Bahn Gondola [S] - Lionshead Circle (970) 476-9090
Gondola rides are always fun for kids, and are an easy way to get to an alpine environment. At the top you can take a hike, have a picnic, or simply bask in the scenery. Adults have to pay, but children under 12 are FREE.

Nature Discovery Center [T] - Top of Eagle Bahn Gondola   (970) 754-4675
www.walkingmountains.org
You have to ride the gondola (or hike up!) to get to the center, but once there visitors can learn about the alpine ecosystem through interactive displays. Guided nature hikes are also available. FREE

photo by Nathan Pulley

Vail   133

Vail Nature Center ᵁ - 601 Vail Valley Drive
(970) 479-2291

They say that the nature center is one of Vail's best kept secrets. It is housed in a log cabin on the banks of Gore Creek, and offers plant and animal exhibits as well as a variety of programs about the mountain environment and guided hikes. $

Directions
Numerous exits along I-70, west of Vail Pass.

Parking
Central parking at the *Vail Village Parking* ⱽ (exit 176). Parking and bus transportation are free during the summer. Shuttles every 10 minutes.

Free parking is also available at the *Lionshead Parking* ᵂ structure

A. Vail Village – from the Vail Village Parking walk south across the covered bridge
B. Betty Ford Alpine Gardens - 530 South Frontage Road (in Ford Park)
C. Red Sandstone Park – over the pedestrian overpass from Lionshead Village, 250 yards west
D. Pirate Ship Park – walk through Vail Village to the base of the mountain
E. Ford Park - 530 South Frontage Road
F. Children's Fountain - Wall St and Gore Creek Dr
G. Joe's Famous Deli - 288 Bridge Street
H. La Cantina - 241 S. Frontage Rd.
I. Loaded Joe's - 227 Bridge Street
J. Moe's Original Bar-B-Que - 616 W. Lionshead
K. Red Lion Restaurant - 304 Bridge Street
L. Imagination Station - 395 East Lionshead Circle
M. City Market - 2109 N Frontage Rd
N. Safeway - 2131 North Frontage Road
O. Vail Public Library - 292 West Meadow Drive
P. Vail Valley Medical Center - 181 W. Meadow Drive
Q. Vail Visitor Information Center - 241 S. Frontage Road (at the Vail Village Parking Structure)
R. Lionshead Information Center - 395 S. Frontage Road (at the LionsHead Parking Structure)
S. Eagle Bahn Gondola - Lionshead Village
T. Nature Discovery Center - Top of Eagle Bahn Gondola
U. Vail Nature Center - 601 Vail Valley Drive
V. Vail Village Parking – 241 S. Frontage Rd.
W. Lionshead Parking – 395 S. Frontage Rd.

Walsenburg

A stop in Walsenburg is a step back in time. Originally settled by Spanish farmers, Walsenburg grew and developed with the discovery of coal in the area. Today it retains its small-town atmosphere and hosts visitors interested in a variety of outdoor adventures nearby.

The Place to Go

City Park [A] - (W 7th and S Olive) This is the easiest stop to make in town. It has a nice playground, shaded benches, picnic tables and public restrooms. However, be warned, the aquatic park is next door...it might be irresistible to travel-weary children.

Another Park

Civic League Park [B] - (Albert Ave and W. 1st St) If you want to stay away from the aquatic park, try Civic League Park, a nice little community park a few blocks off the main drag. There's a playground, shade, picnic shelter, tables, and restrooms.

Splash Spot

Walsenburg Wild Waters Aquatic Park [C]
700 W 7th Street. (719)738-2628
www.cityofwalsenburg.com/waterpark.php
A big surprise in a little town. The aquatic park, opened in 2007, has three pools, giant water slides, interactive water features, a diving board and a lazy river. There's even a zero-entry pool and a small slide for the littlest swimmers. $

Kid-Friendly Eateries
(with something for adults too!)

Corine's Mexican Food [D] - 822 Main Street. (719) 738-1231
If you're looking for Mexican food, this is the place to go in Walsenburg.

George's Drive Inn [E] - 564 US Highway 85-87. (719) 738-3030
Don't be fooled by the unassuming building... this popular restaurant has fresh food and great burgers.

Mike's Coffee Barn [F] - 302 W. 7th Street. (719) 738-3318
Need coffee? Stop here.

Pizza Hut [G] - 973 Hwy 85-87. (719) 738-3783
Pizza, pizza, pizza (and some pasta, too).

Things to do in Bad Weather

Walsenburg Mining Museum [H] - 112 W. 5th Street. (719) 738-1992
This museum is on The National Register of Historic Buildings, and houses exhibits portraying the history of mining in the Walsenburg area. The Huerfano County Historical Society operates the museum, and asks potential visitors to call ahead for hours. $

Walsenburg

Groceries/Supplies

Safeway [I] - 222 West 7th Street. (719) 738-3301.

More Info

Library: Spanish Peaks Library [J] - 415 Walsen Avenue. (719) 738-2774   www.spld.org

Hospital/Emergency Care: *Spanish Peaks Regional Health Center* - 23500 US-160. (719) 738-5100   www.sprhc.org

Visitor's Center [K] - 400 Main Street. (719) 738-1065

Other Fun Stuff

Lathrop State Park [L] - 70 CR 502. (719) 738-2376   http://parks.state.co.us/parks/lathrop/Pages/LathropStatePark.aspx

Lathrop State Park was Colorado's first state park. It sits in the shadow of the Spanish Peaks, and is home to two lakes which offer a variety of water activities, including swimming. The park also has a 2-mile nature trail, as well as a 3-mile paved trail around Martin Lake. $

Directions

From the north or south, use I-25, and follow the I-25 Business Route into town.

From the west, US-160 will bring you into town on W. 7th Street.

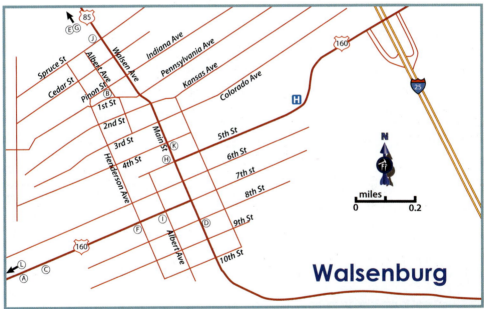

A. City Park – W. 7th & S. Olive
B. Civic League Park – Albert Avenue & W. 1st Street
C. Walsenburg Wild Waters Aquatic Park -700 W 7th Street
D. Corine's Mexican Food - 822 Main St.
E. George's Drive Inn - 564 US Highway 85/87
F. Mike's Coffee Barn - 302 W. 7th St
G. Pizza Hut - 973 US Hwy 85/87
H. Walsenburg Mining Museum -112 W. 5th Street
I. Safeway - 222 West 7th Street
J. Spanish Peaks Library - 415 Walsen Avenue
K. Visitor's Center – 400 Main Street
L. Lathrop State Park - 70 CR 502 (3 miles west of Walsenburg on US-160)

Winter Park

While the resort is certainly large and well-known, the town of Winter Park has managed to retain its small-town atmosphere. Located just west of the Continental Divide at the southern end of the Fraser Valley, Winter Park is full of wide open spaces, wildflowers, aspen, wildlife and adventure.

The Place to Go

Hideaway Park [A] - (On US-40, just north of the Visitor Center) This fairly new playground is strategically located in the heart of Winter Park, along US-40. The play structures will provide hours of energy-expending fun. There are also covered picnic tables, public restrooms, a choice of eateries within walking distance, and access to the *Fraser River Trail*.

Another Park

Wolf Park [B] - (320 Kings Crossing Road) For folks who want to get away from the main drag, this park is tucked away in the trees not far off US-40. There is a playground, sandbox, picnic pavilion, lots of shade, public restrooms, and even the *Wolf Park Alpine Trail*.

Splash Spot

Fraser River - Take a walk along the *Fraser River Trail*, and the kids will surely find a great spot to toss a rock, float a stick, or take off their shoes.

Trails for Strollers & Little Folks

Fraser River Trail - This paved, 5-mile trail connects Winter Park resort with the towns of Winter Park and Fraser. It's a great place to stretch legs and take in the scenery. There are also picnic tables and benches along the way. Access near the resort off Trademark Drive; in town across the street from the *Visitor's Center* [N] next to the Ski Broker (78941 US-40); or in Fraser behind the *Safeway* [J].

Wolf Park Alpine Trail - This short, gravel nature trail isn't long, but it is flat, full of great views, and meanders through the pine forest. Access at *Wolf Park* [B].

Winter Park

Kid-Friendly Eateries
(with something for adults too!)

Crooked Creek Saloon ᶜ - 401 Zerex Street (US-40), Fraser. (970) 726-9250
www.crookedcreeksaloon.com
A funky little place, but it comes highly recommended. They serve breakfast, lunch and dinner with menus to satisfy just about every whim.

Deno's Mountain Bistro ᴰ - 78911 US-40. (970) 726-5332   www.denosmountainbistro.com
Deno's features a varied menu, from steaks to seafood, and bbq ribs to a Cajun sandwich. Beer and cocktails, too!

Hernando's Pizza Pub ᴱ - 78199 US-40 (at the intersection of King's Crossing Road).
(970) 726-5409   www.hernandospizzapub.com
Pizza worth waiting for (and it will be busy!), in an interesting atmosphere. Bring a dollar to add to the wall.

Mountain Grind Coffee & Bistro ᶠ - 47 Cooper Creek Square. (970) 726-0999
www.mountain-grind.com
Not just coffee. The bistro serves soup, sandwiches, pastries and more.

Mountain Rose Café ᴳ - 78542 US-40. (970) 726-1374   www.mountainrosecafe.com
Serving the best breakfast in Winter Park, the Mountain Rose Café claims to have "Redneck mountain fusion with a dash of hippie love."

Rudi's Deli ᴴ - 78699 US-40. (970) 726-8955
www.winterparkdeli.com
Their favorite quote is, "It isn't Winter Park without a stop a Rudi's." And they are oh, so right.

Things to do in Bad Weather

Grand Park Community Recreation Center ᴵ - 1 Main Street, Fraser. (970) 726-8968
www.fraservalleyrec.org/index.php
Drive a couple miles north to Fraser for a great place to expend energy in bad weather. The rec center has a leisure pool with a 20-foot water slide, interactive water features, a lazy river, and zero-depth entry. You'll also find a gym, weight room and track. $

Groceries/Supplies

Safeway ᴶ - 40 County Rd. 804 (along US-40), Fraser. (970) 726-9484

Winter Park Market & Deli ᴷ - 78336 US-40. (970) 726-4704

More Info

Library: Fraser Valley Library ᴸ - 421 Norgren Road, Fraser. (970) 726-5689
www.gcld.org/content/locations/fv

Hospital/Emergency Care: *Denver Health East Grand Clinic* ᴹ - 145 Parsenn Road. (970) 726-4299
http://denverhealth.org/Services/CommunityHeaEastGrandCommunityClinic.aspx

Winter Park-Fraser Valley Visitor Center ᴺ -78841 US-40. (970) 726-4118 OR (800) 903-7275   www.playwinterpark.com

More Info: www.allwinterpark.com
www.winterparkguide.com

Other Fun Stuff

Cozens Ranch Museum ᴼ - 77849 US-40. (970) 726-5488
Cozens Ranch is an 1870s homestead, and affords visitors a step back in time to the pioneer days in Colorado. On the premises are the restored family residence, a hotel, a stagecoach stop and even the original Fraser post office. $

Winter Park Alpine Slide ᴾ - 85 Parsenn Rd. (at the Winter Park base area). (970) 726-1564
www.winterparkresort.com/tickets/summer_rates/index.htm
Winter Park boasts the longest alpine slide in Colorado. Take a scenic ride up on the Arrow chairlift, then whoosh down the mountain (610 vertical feet!). $

Directions

Winter Park is located on US-40, south of Fraser.

Winter Park

A. Hideaway Park – On US-40, just north of the Visitor Center
B. Wolf Park – 320 Kings Crossing Road (.6 miles up the road from US-40)
C. Crooked Creek Saloon - 401 Zerex Street (US-40), Fraser
D. Deno's Mountain Bistro - 78911 US-40
E. Hernando's Pizza Pub - 78199 US-40 (at the intersection of King's Crossing Rd.)
F. Mountain Grind Coffee & Bistro - 47 Cooper Creek Square
G. Mountain Rose Café - 78542 US-40
H. Rudi's Deli - 78699 US-40
I. Grand Park Community Recreation Center – 1 Main Street, Fraser
J. Safeway - 40 County Rd. 804 (along US-40), Fraser
K. Winter Park Market & Deli - 78336 US-40
L. Fraser Valley Library - 421 Norgren Road, Fraser
M. Denver Health East Grand Clinic - 145 Parsenn Rd
N. Winter Park-Fraser Valley Visitor Center – 78841 US-40
O. Cozens Ranch Museum - 77849 US-40
P. Winter Park Alpine Slide – 85 Parsenn Rd. (at the Winter Park base area)

APPENDICES

A - Top 10 Places to Stop and Play

1 - Georgetown – City Park
The play structure at this park is a cross between a fort and a tree house, and will entice even the most travel-weary adult to play.

2 - Sand Dunes
What's to say? It's the largest sandbox ever. And if you're lucky, Medano Creek is flowing, adding water to the fun. Easily hours of entertainment.

3 - Granby Elementary School playground
The enormous wooden play structure in Granby goes on endlessly, with various bridges, climbing spots, hiding places and more.

4 - Fort Collins - City Park
There's so much to do in City Park you could spend the day there: a playground, a miniature train, paddle boat rentals, an outdoor pool, and lots of old shade trees and grass.

5 - Aspen - John Denver Sanctuary
A stop here is both calming and refreshing. Walk among the rocks etched with John Denver's lyrics, then stroll on the Rio Grande Trail or wade in the Roaring Fork River.

6 - Grand Lake – Lakeside Park
The town of Grand Lake itself is a fun place to visit, but add the beach, the lake, boat rentals and the scenery, and it's the perfect place to spend a few hours (or even days!).

7 - Steamboat – Dr. Rich Weiss Park
Just go sit in the river, warmed by the hot springs. It's warm, it's beautiful, it's free, and the kids will love it.

8 - Telluride – Town Park
This is a beautiful park in a beautiful place. Let the kids play at Imagination Station, go fishing in the kids' pond, take a swim at the community pool, or take a leisurely stroll along the San Miguel River Trail.

9 - Vail – Pirate Ship Park
Definitely not the biggest park, but one of the most unique. Play on the pirate ship, then take a walk on the rec path or visit Vail Village.

10 - Silverthorne – Rainbow Park
If it's a huge, modern playground you want, this is it. The park has several large structures, two of which are three stories tall with long, swirly slides.

B - What to Pack

If you have time to read this, you probably already have the car packed. However, in the event that you are reading this before you leave the house, here are a few ideas that have saved other parents:

NORMAL STUFF
- [ ] clothes, jackets, pajamas, etc.
- [ ] diapers and wipes
- [ ] bathing suits, swim tubes, towels (no matter where you're going...if there's water, they'll wanna get in it)
- [ ] an easily accessible change of clothes...for all of you (you never know when a toe dipping might turn into a body dunking)
- [ ] medications
- [ ] a favorite blanket, animal, pillow, etc.
- [ ] stroller and/or kid-carrier backpack
- [ ] hats
- [ ] sunscreen

FOOD STUFF
- [ ] chewy foods that don't make crumbs (nuts are good, too)
- [ ] sippy cup full of water or juice

ENTERTAINMENT STUFF
- [ ] a list of songs you can sing even if you can't sing
- [ ] audio books and fun music
- [ ] real books
- [ ] box 'o toys full of things the kids have never seen; and if you're feeling especially motivated, pack a car box, and a box they can play with at the destination
- [ ] art supplies; a chalkboard (because even if your child "colors" the inside of the car, he or she can clean it off easily with the cloth you pack); a Magna Doodle; or, for more responsible children, a dry erase board is great for drawing and erasing.

THE STUFF YOU MIGHT NOT THINK OF
- [ ] first-aid kit
- [ ] baby gates for the place you're staying (and outlet covers, doorknob thingies)
- [ ] a Pack 'n Play (or other portable crib) for sleeping
- [ ] booster seat or high chair
- [ ] a car-sick kit (bucket, towel, ginger, ginger ale) because there is nothing worse than vomit spewed all over the car when it's 95° outside (trust me)
- [ ] a clean-up kit for the car (Arm & Hammer Odor Eliminator spray for carpets and fabric-usually used to eliminate pet odor, but works very well on kid odor too; Spot Shot; a few rags; etc.)
- [ ] a plastic bag for wet and/or smelly stuff
- [ ] a timer: if you don't already use one with your kids, start now
- [ ] items for bribery

C – Travel Tips

The first thing people will tell you is to plan and organize ahead of time. They will be right. But if they don't have kids, they also don't know that all the planning in the world won't make you prepared. Children can be very unpredictable. Thus, this book.

Here are a few things fellow parents have learned:

1 - Be prepared. For the unexpected. And just go with it.

2 - Have a flexible time schedule.

3 - Make stopping along the way part of the fun.

4 - Start traveling with your kids when they're itty-bitty (no matter how scary that might be).

5 - Break the rules (try not to stress about schedules, eating junk food, etc.)…you're on vacation and so are they.

6 - Find non-crumby snacks (even if they aren't usually allowed to eat in the car). Think raisins, almonds and chewy snacks.

7 - Create a toy box they can have in the car with them. Many stores even sell boxes specifically for this purpose; the box sits on the child's lap and serves as a writing or play surface as well as a container. Let older kids pack the box.

8 - Pack new a toy(s) or something the kids haven't played with in a while and bring it out in a time of desperation.

9 - Tie everything to the car seat because whether intentional or not, a toy on the floor means you have to contort yourself into strange positions (if you're not driving) to pick it up. Especially savvy parents even pack extra toys up front with them to avoid the contortionist act.

10 - For parents with young children that will sleep in the car, start your road trip right at nap time so the child can sleep and you can get a few miles of travel in peace.

11 - Learn to sing. Loudly.

12 - Don't be afraid of bribery.

13 - Invest in ear plugs.

14 - Buy (ahead of time) a State Parks pass. There are 42 great parks across Colorado, and many are located in remote places where you might find the need for a stop. (www.parks.state.co.us)

15 - If appropriate, involve your kids in the entire process, from the planning to the packing, to the snacks you'll take and where you'll stop.

D - Games You Can Play

All of the games listed below can be varied depending on the age, ability and interests of everyone in the car. They are meant not only as a distraction, but also as a way to have fun as you pass the miles.

1 - Do You See What I See?

This game has many variations, limited only by imagination. For young children, have them look for something red (or blue, or big, or new, etc.). Make the objects more difficult to find as the kids get older. Another option is to have one person pick an object (a digger, a barn, a fence, etc.), then everyone in the car tries to be the first person to spot it; when they do, they shout out the name of the object.

2 - Scavenger Hunt

Scavenger Hunts are great because you can make up the list of items to find right on the spot, and you can make the lists easy or difficult depending on the ability of your children. As a variation, you can also add numbers to the mix (for example, find 3 red cars, 2 fire trucks and one partridge in a pear tree). With young children you can check things off the list together; older children can have their own list and make a contest out of it. Treats for the winner.

<u>In the car</u> - make a list (or draw one with the art supplies you packed!) of 5 things to look for along the road. Ideas include: dump truck, mountain, a red car, a tunnel, a bridge, a stop sign, a train, a school bus, a lake, an animal or a police car.

<u>During your stop</u> - this is a great way to keep kids moving, especially if you want to go on a "hike". Ideas include: something green, rough, new, skinny, round, patterned, or a piece of trash.

<u>In the grocery store (or restaurant)</u> - this is for the very desperate. However, a scavenger hunt can keep kids focused and active. Ideas include: a sweet treat, a lunch item, a vegetable, a fruit, a baked good, a canned good, something cold, a drink or a snack food item (in essence, you're letting the kids do the shopping for you!). In a restaurant, vary the list according to the ambiance. And, of course, the kids will have to stay in their seats, so items must be easily visible.

3 - The Quiet Game (this one's for my dad)

The idea is to see who can be quiet the longest. Winner gets a treat (this is why you brought those items for bribery – Appendix B). Winner gets a treat. You can also see if everyone can be quiet for 5 miles (or 10 or 20...), then dole out treats and up the ante.

4 - The Cloud Game

You'll need clouds for this one, so wait for a great puffy-cloud day. Have everyone stare out the window and use their imagination. What do the clouds look like? A two headed horse? A dancing clown? Points and/or treats for best descriptions (encourage kids to describe things as much as possible).

5 - Alphabet Game
This is a great game for kids that know their alphabet and even for kids just learning. First, find something (or several things) that start with an A (automobile, asphalt, apple, etc.). Then proceed through the alphabet. For kids that are learning their letters and sounds, this offers a great teaching opportunity while having fun, too!

6 - Count That
One player picks an item they will count (but doesn't tell anyone). Then, as the player sees that object, they count out loud. Everyone else in the car tries to guess what is being counted. The person to guess correctly counts next. For very young children, select something to count as a group, and count out loud together.

7 - Make Noise!
Everyone in the car takes a turn making a noise. Then everyone else tries to name as many things as they can that make that noise (for example, things that howl include the wind, a wolf or a kid having a fit). Noise ideas: snap, roar, thump, bang, knock, tap, drip, squeak, rumble and hiss.

8 - What was your favorite?
This isn't as much a game as it is a discussion and an exercise in memory. Nonetheless, it is great for the ride home. Everyone in the car takes a turn answering the question, "What was your favorite part of the trip?" The question refers to the trip and all the fun things you've done. To extend the game, have everyone tell their three favorites, or ask more specific questions such as, "What was your favorite meal?" or "What was your favorite activity?" or "What was your favorite stopping spot?" Parents need to answer the questions, too!

9 - Follow Me
If you need a physical outlet while still in the car, try this one. One passenger performs an action, such as patting their head. The next person repeats that action, and adds their own, such as snapping. The third person then pats their head, snaps their fingers and adds a third action. The game continues until someone slips up, but then you get to start again! Part of the fun of this game is coming up with creative actions. For small children, try a simple game of Simon Says.

10 - Story Time
Write a story together! Even very young children can participate in this with guidance. The person that starts the story might say, "Once upon a time, there was a turtle who lived in a pond." Then the next person adds the story. "The turtle's name was Leo, and he was very lonely." Some stores even sell cards with images specifically for this purpose. Or, bring cards from a memory game or pictures cut from a magazine to propel the story forward. You can use just one picture, or continue holding up new pictures if kids need help coming up with ideas.

Why I Wrote This Book (the true story)

Anyone who's ever had a kid knows that even the best travelers have bad days. And anyone who's ever traveled with a kid in the car, be it for 5 minutes or 5 hours, understands what a "bad day" really looks like. Enough said.

My twin boys are generally good travelers. Not much fussing, not needy. They just go with the flow. Except one afternoon the summer they were two. We'd already had several great road trips that summer, so The Horrid Trip was unexpected. We were on our way home from a fantastic long weekend, a 2-3 hour drive. No problem.

However, somewhere between Unmentioned Town A and Unmentioned Town B, we had a double melt-down of epic proportions. It started slowly, allowing us to (stupidly) think we could make it to Town B with our sanity in tact. With Town A barely out of sight in the rear-view mirror, the storm gathered force. But we only had 30 miles to go! We could make it!

With 25 miles to go, the meltdown reached category 5, times two (actually, it's exponential...so a category 5 meltdown, raised to the 2nd power). Vowing never to go on a family vacation again, we tried everything (oh, I mean everything) to calm the uncalmable. We offered toys. We rolled windows up and down. We offered food (something we NEVER did in the car). And finally, we sang. My husband and I are not good singers, but we were rock stars that day, singing a hundred iterations of "Wheels on the Bus." It sort-of worked. The storm abated to a category 3.

If you've ever traveled with children you understand how stress builds in a car. How the stress grows, and then takes on a force all its own. It seeps into your skin, your bones, your blood...even your hair. Your grip on the steering wheel is so tight you might actually crush it, or find the need for someone to surgically remove your fingers from the wheel when you (finally) stop. Was I speeding? You bet. So when Town B loomed brilliantly on the horizon, we felt a smidgeon of hope. We'd made it!

But where to stop? I had never seen a park in that town. I didn't know if there was a creek nearby, or even a spot of grass. We didn't need much. BUT WE HAD TO GET OUT! Stress drove the car at that point. It squealed us (on two wheels) into the first parking lot we saw. Didn't matter that there was nothing there but gravel, trash and broken glass. WE HAD TO GET OUT! And we didn't know where else to go.

I cursed Town B for a long time. I vowed never to go back. Ever. But, while doing my research for this book, I found that Town B actually has GREAT places to stop, and one of the coolest playgrounds in Colorado.

So, this book was written for all those parents, like myself, who had never considered where the kid-friendly spots are in towns across Colorado. I knew the coffee shops. The breweries. And now, thankfully, all the places to stop with kids.

Happy trails.